ADVENTURING WITH KIDS

ADVENTURING WITH KIDS

GLACIER
NATIONAL PARK

HARLEY AND ABBY MCALLISTER

MOUNTAINEERS
BOOKS

MOUNTAINEERS BOOKS is the publishing division of The Mountaineers, an organization founded in 1906 and dedicated to the exploration, preservation, and enjoyment of outdoor and wilderness areas.

1001 SW Klickitat Way, Suite 201 • Seattle, WA 98134
800.553.4453 • www.mountaineersbooks.org

Printed in China
Distributed in the United Kingdom by Cordee, www.cordee.co.uk
First edition, 2018

Copyeditor: Erin Moore
Design and layout: Heidi Smets
Cartographer: Lohnes+Wright
All photographs by the authors unless credited otherwise.
Cover photograph: *Mountain goat on Logan Pass* (sboice/iStock)
Page 208 photograph: *Young mountain goat* (NPS/Tim Rains)

Library of Congress Cataloging-in-Publication data is on file for this title.

Mountaineers Books titles may be purchased for corporate, educational, or other promotional sales, and our authors are available for a wide range of events. For information on special discounts or booking an author, contact our customer service at 800-553-4453 or mbooks@mountaineersbooks.org.

ISBN (paperback): 978-1-68051-116-1
ISBN (ebook): 978-1-68051-117-8

CONTENTS

Pristine waterfalls are one of the many jewels in the Crown of the Continent.

INTRODUCTION

No other national park is described as "The Crown of the Continent," and for good reason. It's not just that Glacier sits atop the Continental Divide and is one of the highest elevation parks in the United States. One journey over the historic Going-to-the-Sun Road will convince you that Glacier National Park is also a jewel in the national park system. With glaciers, grizzlies, and jagged peaks, Glacier is unmatched; but this can also make it a bit intimidating to plan an adventure with kids in mind.

The glaciers exist here not only as remnants of the last Ice Age, but also because it is high and cold; the weather here can suddenly turn harsh and frigid any month of the year, often with little or no warning. Although this means that you can see a stunning display of wildflowers even late in the summer on the top of Logan Pass, it also creates a challenge for keeping your kids warm and happy.

Glacier is big and wild, which results in it having the highest density of bears in the Lower 48. And because it sits at the very top of the Lower 48, Glacier National Park shares a border with Waterton Lakes National Park in Alberta, Canada. Sharing a border means that many animals can make their way down into Glacier and back again. The shared border enlarges the park as an ecosystem, and it's another feature that makes Glacier special.

Wildlife here is up close and personal. You will likely see snowy-white mountain goats, and watch their kids nimbly hopping from rock to rock ahead of you. Maybe you will spot a moose feeding nearby in a shallow lake where they feel safe from predators. Or quite possibly you will round a corner on a trail and stop dead in your tracks at the sight of a bear tearing up the ground, searching for grubs or a ground squirrel. While exhilarating to see, these wild animals can also spell danger, especially for children who are not always as aware of what is around them as you are. At Glacier in particular, it's important to go into your hikes and adventures aware that wild animals deserve distance and respect; they can be unpredictable.

While these observations are not meant to scare you off, they should give you pause. Glacier is a deeply wild place, mostly untamed. A trip to this national park requires careful thought and planning before venturing out with your kids, and this book was written to help you with just that challenge. We have taken our four children with us on multiple trips around Glacier and they have loved it. Our four-year-old asks us every week when we're going back to Glacier National Park. It is our hope that this book will help you plan and execute the amazing family vacation you dream of.

TOP FIVE TIPS FOR VACATIONING IN GLACIER WITH KIDS

Over the years, we have traveled to well over a dozen national parks with our kids, and these experiences have taught us many lessons. Foremost among those is the realization that kids learn about and relate to the environment differently than adults do, so we've developed recommendations for adventuring with kids with an eye toward getting them to deeply engage with their surroundings.

Here are our top five tips for making the most of your family vacation.

1. Get out of the car.

Glacier abounds in astounding sights, but the views along Going-to-the-Sun Road are beyond description. This 50-mile-long marvel of engineering bisects Glacier National Park and carries you through every type of terrain and ecosystem found in the park. For many adults, just driving the highway without hiking is sufficient. In truth, our kids also thought this was one

A visit to Glacier National Park offers sights like this moose feeding in the evening.

You may encounter some wild bighorn along the trail to Appistoki Falls in the Two Medicine Region.

of the most enjoyable roads we've ever traveled. Still, simply driving Going-to-the-Sun Road won't impart the lasting memories and lessons that foot travel always does—especially for children.

To build memories that your family can share for years to come, and to create a sense of responsibility and stewardship toward places like Glacier, nothing beats hitting the trail. Your kids need to engage all of their senses while exploring. They need to smell the damp and fecund forest as they run down the trail. They should feel the exhilaration of crossing a log bridge over a river filled with whitewater and hear the sounds of the animals around them when they stop for a snack along the way. These are the experiences that will make your family trip to Glacier indelibly written on their minds.

If that task seems daunting, read on. We are here to help you on that journey, and we promise it will be worth it for both you and your kids!

2. Download your digital content prior to departure.

The remoteness of Glacier and its soaring heights means that wireless and cellular coverage is spotty or nonexistent. Some of the lodges do have Wi-Fi access and cell coverage, but it is not something you can count on. So, if you expect to use the internet to plan your vacation once you arrive there, you will be out of luck. Make sure all the resources you want to use are downloaded ahead of time. Remember that this goes for digital content that you may want for your kids while the family is trapped in the car—although we limit device use with our kids now that they are older and better able to appreciate the sights out the window. You won't be able to stream videos or music for the kiddos, so download what you think they will need ahead of time. A good compromise on the device debate is to use audiobooks. You can download digital audiobooks from many places, including for free from most local libraries. Your kids have something to listen to, but they can also still look out the window.

3. Have a plan B.

Glacier is subject to profoundly fickle weather. Within minutes it can change from sunny and warm to cold and rainy, so it is a good idea to have a plan B. One of our favorite plan Bs is to scoot on over to the nearest historic lodge when the weather gets bad; there are several in the park. One year, we waited out a wet, cold storm by hunkering down in the Many Glacier Hotel in the Many Glacier Region. We brought in our own snacks, plus a deck of cards; purchased mugs of hot chocolate from the little store on the floor below; and claimed a comfy seating arrangement near the huge picture windows in the lobby area. We watched from our couches as the storm rolled over the mountains and across the lake. It hit the lodge and blew past as

Indoor exhibits, like these at the Apgar Visitor Center, are good rainy-day distractions. (NPS/David Restivo photo)

we played another round of cards. Once the weather passed, we cleaned up our little sanctuary and headed outside. This is an especially great strategy if you are tent camping.

Another alternative plan that we use is to save poking around the visitor centers until the weather gets bad. As trained teachers, we know that if you want kids engaged in content and retaining new information, you need to activate their prior knowledge and experience. This means that your kids will get much more out of the information offered at national park visitor centers if they have firsthand experience in the park first. Therefore, we always recommend stopping in to look at the interpretive exhibits and watch the movie *after* you have been hiking and exploring in the park. The only exception we make to this rule is for bad weather. However, you will find that many other visitors also use the visitor centers as rain shelters, so it can be crowded at these times. It's a good idea to keep an eye on your children.

One more alternative to hiking during a day of inclement weather is to avail yourself of the park's free "hop on, hop off" shuttle service (see Resources). We actually stumbled into this plan one day as we were finishing a hike in the St. Mary and Logan Pass Region. About a quarter of a mile out from the trailhead, it began to pour rain. We sprinted for the road, but unfortunately our car was parked another mile farther on. A shuttle bus happened to stop right as we came off the trail, and although it was heading *away* from our car, we hopped on anyway to escape the storm. We ended up riding it all the way to Logan Pass and then transferred to the "going down" shuttle for a trip back to our car.

Of course, you could also go for a drive in your own car, but the shuttle saves you (and the planet) gas, and our young kids enjoyed the thrills of this adventure, as only young kids can!

4. Start easy and leave extra time.

With "get out of the car" we encouraged you to get outside; now we're going to caution you to take it easy. With kids, make your first hike or outing less challenging than later ones, so that they don't get discouraged right off the bat. And allow extra time because, unlike adults, who are often focused on making it to the destination, kids are much more interested in enjoying the journey. Make sure to leave ample time for breaks, stopping to check out a creek or flower along the way, or anything else that might pop up. Kids want time to explore, and it is up to you to leave time in the schedule for them to discover new things. This book's hike descriptions list a wide range of times to complete each hike, and that is because it depends on so many factors: age, fitness level, number of breaks for snacks or picnics, and time allowed for exploration. Use your first few shorter outings to get a feel for how fast you hike as a family unit and then use that knowledge to better estimate the longer hikes.

Don't forget to take time for snack breaks!

5. Bring plenty of the essentials.

If young people are not enjoying themselves outside, it is almost always due to one of two things—they are hungry or otherwise uncomfortable (chilled, overheated, sore feet). Bring plenty of water, plus trail mix, granola, nuts, fruit, and even candy bars. I've lost count of the number of times we've been out with our kids and they started getting grouchy and whining, only to take a five-minute snack break and have them back in high spirits and raring to go. Napoleon Bonaparte once said that "an army marches on its stomach," and this is even more true of children.

Secondly, being outside means being exposed to the elements. This brings adventure but also risks, so be prepared. We always carry an extra fleece jacket or sweatshirt with us, even on short hikes, and we bring rain gear on medium or longer jaunts. Sunscreen is also wise: Glacier's high elevation means higher levels of UV rays and more chance of sunburn. More detailed checklists come later in the book, but food, water, and protection against the elements are always the most important items.

Experiencing Baring Falls in the St. Mary and Logan Pass Region is well worth the hike.

HOW TO USE THIS BOOK

Our family has enjoyed our many visits to Glacier National Park, and we want this book to help you plan vacations that will result in memories your family will cherish for years to come.

We've chosen family-focused hikes and activities emphasizing kids and what they like to see and do. We also keep in mind what adults like, selecting hikes that are friendly for kids, sure, but also enjoyable for parents and guardians. Hikes and adventures are arranged by region. Each regional chapter includes a single detailed map featuring recommended hiking trails, distances, campsites, and more. We strongly suggest that you purchase a packet of four regional maps at the first ranger station or visitor center you pass when you arrive at the park. These little maps fit easily into your pocket but provide more detail than the larger maps and make navigating the hiking trails much clearer.

In the descriptions, we've given specifics for what we ourselves have researched. For many hikes, you can go farther or start at a different trailhead; park sources will help you discover more as you build your Glacier adventures (see Resources). Our goal is to help you plan a successful Glacier trip by providing tips for vacationing, sample itineraries, best bets, hiking, and "adventures beyond hiking"—all with families in mind.

This enchanting gorge in the Lake McDonald Region leads you onward and upward to Avalanche Lake.

PLANNING YOUR GLACIER FAMILY VACATION

Planning any sort of trip comes down to a few basic questions: Where you'll go and when you'll go, how you'll get there and where you'll stay, and what you'll do while you're there. In the following pages, we will give you some ideas about what time of year is best in Glacier and itinerary options for how long you want to stay. We'll also give guidance on the best way to get your family to the park, and we will address the question about where to stay in two sections on camping and other lodging options.

The really fun part is filling in your itinerary with exciting adventures! This book aims to give you all the information you need to create a journey that will engage and excite your children and build wonderful memories to last a lifetime.

Part of the Rocky Mountains and spanning the Continental Divide, Glacier National Park is over 1 million acres in size, which makes it both amazing and a bit daunting to visit. The main access is the remarkable Going-to-the-Sun Road. To help make the planning more manageable, we approach the park by region, highlighting hikes, sights, and activities in each. Depending on the length of your trip, the text can help you decide which region to focus on, or perhaps help you plan time to visit all of them:

o **LAKE MCDONALD.** A heavily forested region that offers many activities easily accessible from Going-to-the-Sun Road
o **ST. MARY** includes Logan Pass (the high point on Going-to-the-Sun Road)
o **MANY GLACIER** offers several lodging options and many wonderful trails into the alpine region, with viewing opportunities for some of the more well-known glaciers in the park

Wildflowers are one of the many attractions of Glacier National Park.

- ○ **TWO MEDICINE.** A less visited portion of the park that offers the most solitude of all the regions while still delivering all of the stirring features that draw visitors to Glacier National Park

WHEN TO GO

The season for enjoying most of Glacier National Park is short. Glacier gets a tremendous amount of snow, and from October through May, snow often closes Going-to-the-Sun Road, leaving only June through September to visit. And even in summer you will be risking cold temperatures (especially at night) and possibly snow, which makes tent camping an especially challenging adventure.

Glacier's high elevation and high latitude bring good things too. During the peak season, late June through August, spring wildflowers will almost always be blooming somewhere in the park, first in the lower parts of the park around Lake McDonald and St. Mary and by August on the top of Logan Pass. This is an extraordinary aspect of Glacier seldom experienced in other places.

Historic snowplow opening dates for Going-to-the-Sun Road, kept by the park service, help you plan a window of time when main valleys, roads, and campgrounds will most likely be accessible. Check out Glacier National Park's website and look for any alerts in effect. You can also find campground and lodging information with opening and closing dates. Reviewed together, these will help you choose an optimal window of time for your family's visit. As your trip gets closer, use an online weather forecasting tool to make last-minute adjustments to your plans. Some of our favorites include Weather Underground and NOAA (see Resources).

GETTING THERE

Keep in mind as you plan your trip that Glacier is located in a fairly remote corner of Montana. You will need to accurately calculate travel time to and from the park, whether you are

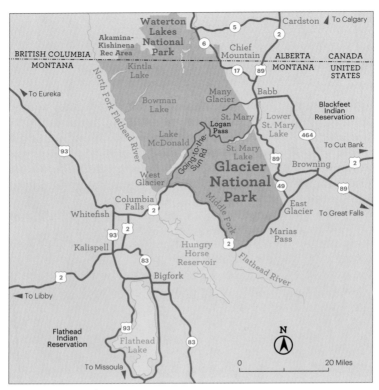

Legend

──15──	Interstate Highway
──89──	US Highway
──24──	State Highway
──────	Other Road
-------	Dirt Road
-------	Main Trail
-------	Other Trail

🅐	Picnic Area
▪	Point of Interest
Ⓐ	Campground
❶	Ranger Station
Ⓟ	Parking
∿	River
	Lake
	Park

Map labels:

Waterton Lakes National Park
Akamina-Kishinena Rec Area
Cardston — To Calgary
Chief Mountain
BRITISH COLUMBIA
MONTANA
ALBERTA — CANADA
MONTANA — UNITED STATES
To Eureka
Kintla Lake
Bowman Lake
Many Glacier
Babb
Blackfeet Indian Reservation
St. Mary
Logan Pass
Lower St. Mary Lake
Lake McDonald
To Cut Bank
St. Mary Lake
North Fork Flathead River
Going-to-the-Sun Rd
Glacier National Park
West Glacier
Browning
Columbia Falls
Whitefish
East Glacier
To Great Falls
Kalispell
Middle Fork
Marias Pass
Hungry Horse Reservoir
Bigfork
Flathead River
To Libby
Flathead Indian Reservation
Flathead Lake
To Missoula

N

0 — 20 Miles

driving a personal vehicle from home to the park or flying in to a local city and renting a vehicle there. A fun option to consider is taking the train. Before booking your travel, consider which side of the park you will visit, the east or the west, or, if both, where you will start and finish. Keep in mind that, while stunning to drive—and the only road that crosses the park—Going-to-the-Sun Road is slow, with loops and turns and elevation gained and lost. If you will be arriving and departing from the same side of the park, as most visitors do, you'll need to schedule plenty of time to cross the park or drive around its southern border. (State Highway 2, which brings you to the west entrance, continues on around the south side of the park.) While it's nice to have options for traveling to the other side of the park, we didn't find any significant time advantage to either route.

By Air

For access to the west side of the park, the nearest airport is just outside Kalispell, Montana, 30 miles west of the Apgar Visitor Center and western park entrance. A slightly bigger airport is located in Missoula, Montana, but that is 150 miles from the west entrance. There are rental car services at both airports. From Kalispell a shuttle service can take you into the park, but normally a family will need to rent a car in order to comfortably and easily complete a reasonable itinerary.

Another option: If you will be arriving from the east, the Great Falls, Montana, airport is 130 to 165 miles away—depending on which of the eastern entrances you visit first (St. Mary, Two Medicine, or Many Glacier)—and of course you can rent a car at this airport as well.

By Car or RV

If you plan to arrive from the west, you will need to make your way to Kalispell. From there drive 33 miles on Highway 2 north to West Glacier and on into the park. Alternatively, from July 1 to September 5, you can usually catch a shuttle from Whitefish, Montana, but be aware that early snows can sometimes force earlier closures. Learn more at Glacier Park Express (see Resources).

If you plan to enter via any of the three eastern entrances, you will want to make your way to Browning, Montana, about 125 miles from Great Falls. Once in Browning, follow the signs that will lead you to your desired entrance.

A note on using an RV: We are mostly a tent camping family and often encourage others to give it a try. It is an adventuresome and affordable option. Frankly, though, Glacier National Park can be a difficult place to camp with a family. First, the weather can change suddenly and change often. If you are in the park for three or more days, you are likely to experience cold, rain, and even snow. If you get caught in a storm while on the trail, it's difficult to dry off and warm up in a tent. Also, passing the night in a tent with children while a storm rages can be less than enjoyable—although it can make for good memories years later! Second, the very presence of bears near your campground, both black and grizzly bears, can put an end to your whole trip. If you have a tent camping reservation and the National Park Service feels that a certain bear is overly pesky in your reserved campground, they will cancel your reservation—often without enough time for you to make a different reservation. Glacier is one park where we recommend families rent an RV! See more about bears in the Safety in the Park chapter.

By Train

Finally, you might consider riding the historic Empire Builder train to Glacier National Park. It stops year round at West Glacier and seasonally at East Glacier. Glacier National Park Lodges provides a fee-based shuttle bus from the West Glacier Amtrak station to Apgar Village and Lake McDonald Lodge. The train is a wonderful way to travel with children! Find out more about riding the rails at Amtrak and more about the park's

"Trails and Rails" program at the Glacier National Park website (see Resources).

SUGGESTED ITINERARIES

Planning a trip to a national park is often challenging. For example, without having been there before, how can you get a true sense of how long it will take to visit various locations? Is it possible to drive from one side of the park to the other in a single day? Where should you stay and how should you organize your hikes and adventures? Below are sample itineraries for various trip lengths, from one to seven days. We hope they will give you an idea of how you might plan your time in Glacier. Because there are several entrance points to the park, rather than saying "Day One, Day Two," and so on, we simply state how long you should spend in each region. That way you can move the days around in a way that suits you and your family. Use the following itineraries as customizable guides to fit your situation and the activities you are most looking forward to. You'll find "must-see-and-do" attractions, as well as lodging options. Overnight options are detailed in the Camping and Lodging chapter. These itineraries exclude travel time getting to Glacier.

You really can't see a park as big as Glacier in one day; even two days allows you to only scratch the surface. But if you just don't have any other option, select from the three-day itineraries below to plan a one- or two-day itinerary. Make your choices based on where you will enter and exit the park. There are four entrances, each corresponding to a region. Because Glacier Park is roughly divided into two parts—east and west—along the spine of the Continental Divide, for a one-day itinerary you will have to choose a side to spend your time in. Going-to-the-Sun Road is a must for any visit to Glacier, so no matter which side you settle on, plan time to at least drive to the summit at Logan Pass. You'll get a feel for the immensity of the park along this marvel of a road. Just remember: your kids likely won't remember much if all you do is drive, no matter how impressive the scenery. Make time to get out and hike, and suddenly the day is punctuated with adventure and meaning.

3 Three-Day Itinerary

Frankly, three days is the minimum amount of time we recommend for a visit to Glacier, giving you a good feel for the park yet leaving you wanting to return for more. Consider which entrance you'll use to arrive and depart, and move the days in your itinerary around to fit your plan. Keep in mind that much of Going-to-the-Sun Road, the only road that traverses the park, is posted as 35 miles an hour, and it takes a very long time to drive between Lake McDonald and St. Mary. It's best to camp or stay overnight on the side of the park, whether west or east, that you plan on visiting for that day. With a three-day itinerary, it is possible to base your family out of one east-side region and visit the remaining two east-side portions with day trips. This involves more time in the car but saves you from having to move camp or lodging, which also takes time. Finally, we think that if you only have time for a short visit, you will get the most accurate representation of the park by choosing Glacier's east side for your adventures, making the long drive and substituting in an alternate day at Lake McDonald if you would really like to experience the west side too.

St. Mary and Logan Pass Region: 1 Day

Must-See-and-Do Attractions

- Going-to-the-Sun Road to Logan Pass by car or free shuttle service offered by the park from the St. Mary Visitor Center or nearby lodges
- Hidden Lake Overlook (to just beyond where the boardwalk ends): 45 minutes
- Highline Trail (past the cliffside areas to the "Garden Wall," then return): 1 hour
- Picnic lunch outside the visitor center

Logan Pass Visitor Center on a stormy day

- o Going-to-the-Sun Road back to the Virginia Falls trailhead stop
- o Virginia and St. Mary Falls: 3–4 hours

Lodging Options
Plan to stay in the St. Mary and Logan Pass Region.
- o St. Mary Campground
- o Rising Sun Campground
- o Rising Sun Motor Inn & Cabins

Logan Pass is prime wildlife habitat, and hiking even a portion of the trails along the pass gives you and your children extraordinary opportunities to see diverse wildlife (for example, along Hidden Lake Overlook Trail) and encounter glacial-carved rock, steep terrain, and alpine ecosystems (along the Highline Trail). You'll experience the eastern portion of Going-to-the-Sun Road with a drive that saves time for other activities in the lower elevations of the region.

Many Glacier Region: 1 Day

Must-See-and-Do Attractions

o Redrock Falls with a stop at Fishercap Lake on the way: 3.5 hours
o Swiftcurrent Nature Trail: 2 hours

Lodging Options

Either stay in the St. Mary and Logan Pass Region and "commute" in, or choose a Many Glacier option.

o Many Glacier Campground
o Many Glacier Hotel; Swiftcurrent Motor Inn & Cabins

The Many Glacier Region offers great opportunities to see moose, especially at Fishercap Lake and at the top of Swiftcurrent Lake along the Swiftcurrent Nature Trail. The hike to Redrock Falls takes you through gorgeous scenery and to a beautiful waterfall. Or replace the nature trail with boat rides over Swiftcurrent Lake and Lake Josephine. Even if you don't have time to hike beyond the shores of Josephine, the boat rides are still wonderful.

The Many Glacier Region includes some great falls.

McDonald Creek emptying into Lake McDonald

Two Medicine Region: 1 Day

Must-See-and-Do Attractions

You have a couple of options to fill a day in the Two Medicine Region. Either:

o Running Eagle/Trick Falls: 45 minutes
o Aster Falls (with option to push on to Rockwell Falls): 4 hours (5.5–6 hours)

Or

o Boat ride across Two Medicine Lake, 45 minutes, with one of the following hikes from the east end of the lake:
  o Rockwell Falls: 3 hours
  o Upper Two Medicine Lake with a stop at Twin Falls: 3 hours
o Boat ride back to west side boat dock

Lodging Options

Either stay in the St. Mary and Logan Pass Region and "commute" in, or stay in the Two Medicine area.

o Two Medicine Campground

This region offers for some interesting itineraries based on the boat system, which offers quick access to more remote hikes, like Rockwell Falls and Upper Two Medicine Lake. For example, the hike to Rockwell Falls can be done either as an out-and-back hike or by taking the boat across Two Medicine Lake and hiking from there.

Lake McDonald Region: Optional 1 Day

Must-See-and-Do Attractions

o Avalanche Lake: 3 hours

o Trail of the Cedars: 40 minutes

o McDonald Creek and McDonald Falls, starting near the Johns Lake trailhead and heading down toward Lake McDonald: 1 hour

Lodging Options

o Fish Creek Campground; Sprague Creek Campground; Avalanche Campground

o Village Inn at Apgar; Apgar Village Lodge & Cabins; Lake McDonald Lodge, Cabins & Suites; Motel Lake McDonald

If you are sticking to Glacier's eastside regions, it makes sense to either home base out of St. Mary, driving each day to either of the other two regions, or to change lodging each night, for example starting in the north in Many Glacier, then moving on to St. Mary and Logan Pass, and finally to Two Medicine. When substituting in the Lake McDonald one-day option in your three-day itinerary, we recommend building it in at either the beginning or the end of your trip, and staying the first or final night in the Lake McDonald Region. Driving Going-to-the-Sun Road twice in one day is agony for kids; this way you drive it only once.

Five-Day Itinerary

If you are able to take an entire week for your vacation, your family can experience Glacier in a deeper way. Assuming you will travel on the bookend weekends and have five full days in the park, here are our suggested activities. Remember, switch the days around in a way that makes sense based on where you plan to arrive and depart.

St. Mary and Logan Pass Region: 1 Day

Must-See-and-Do Attractions

Make your way to Logan Pass by car or by the free shuttle system.

o Hidden Lake Overlook (to just beyond where the boardwalk ends): 45 minutes

Little Columbian ground squirrels live in some very big country.

- Highline Trail (past the cliffside areas to the "Garden Wall," then return): 1 hour
- Picnic lunch outside the visitor center
- Return down Going-to-the-Sun Road to the Virginia Falls trailhead
- Virginia and St. Mary Falls hike: 3–4 hours

Lodging Options
Plan to stay in St. Mary.
- St. Mary Campground; Rising Sun Campground
- Rising Sun Motor Inn & Cabins

By hiking only a portion of the trails on Logan Pass, you will get the chance to see prime wildlife habitat and hopefully the wildlife itself (Hidden Lake Overlook) as well as alpine terrain (Highline Trail) while saving time for other activities in the lower elevations of St. Mary. This also gives you a chance to see the eastern portion of Going-to-the-Sun Road.

Many Glacier: 2 days

Must-See-and-Do Attractions
o Redrock Falls with a stop at Fishercap Lake on the way: 3.5 hours
o Swiftcurrent Nature Trail: 2 hours
o Boat ride to the top of Lake Josephine, hike to Grinnell Glacier or Grinnell Lake: 4.5 hours

Lodging Options
Either stay in the St. Mary and Logan Pass Region and "commute" in, or choose a Many Glacier Region option.
o Many Glacier Campground
o Many Glacier Hotel; Swiftcurrent Motor Inn & Cabins

Grinnell Glacier is a definite "don't-miss" for strong hikers!

FIRE!

One universal law about the natural world is that it is in a constant state of flux. Conditions can—and will—change, sometimes gradually and sometimes suddenly. Wildfires are increasing in frequency and ferocity all over the American West, and that includes Glacier National Park. As this book was being prepared, the Sprague Fire destroyed the Sperry Chalet—and affected the surrounding trails and land. Following fires, burned areas are typically closed, at least temporarily, to allow soils to stabilize and to protect the public. It is important to check with a ranger station to make sure the route is open before heading out on any trails.

Two Medicine: 2 days

Must-See-and-Do Attractions
o Running Eagle/Trick Falls: 45 minutes
o Aster Falls (with option to push on to Rockwell Falls): 4 hours (5.5–6 hours)
o Boat ride across Two Medicine Lake and hike to Upper Two Medicine Lake with a stop at Twin Falls: 45 minutes (one-way boat ride), 2–2.5 hours (hike)
o Return by boat to Two Medicine west end boat dock: 45 minutes
o Appistoki Falls: 1 hour
o Pray Lake relaxation: 1 hour or more

Lodging Options
Either stay in the St. Mary and Logan Pass Region and "commute" in, or stay in the Two Medicine area.
o Two Medicine Campground

Like Many Glacier, the Two Medicine area boasts lots of wildlife, but it also has fewer people. The addition of the hike to Appistoki Falls

Stunning Avalanche Lake is surrounded by waterfalls too.

provides a great opportunity to see bighorn sheep. We highly recommend staying at the campground in this area and letting your kids play along the banks of the adjacent Pray Lake. Even if you aren't camping here, it makes a great place to sit, relax, daydream, and skip stones.

Lake McDonald Region: Optional 1 Day

Must-See-and-Do Attractions
- Avalanche Lake hike: 3 hours
- Trail of the Cedars: 40 minutes
- McDonald Creek and McDonald Falls, starting near the Johns Lake trailhead: 1 hour

Lodging Options
- Fish Creek Campground; Apgar Campground; Sprague Creek Campground; Avalanche Campground
- Village Inn at Apgar; Apgar Village Lodge & Cabins; Lake McDonald Lodge, Cabins & Suites; Motel Lake McDonald

If you are excited about seeing the west side of the park, trade this optional day with one of those at either Many Glacier or Two Medicine. If you can, take the hike to Avalanche Lake with a park ranger. They offer keen interpretive information about the natural events occurring in the park.

Seven Days and Beyond

If you are fortunate enough to stay in the park for a week or more, you are very fortunate indeed! Our recommendations for seven days will look a lot like those for five-day trips, with time to add the Lake McDonald Region and even a bit more adventure.

For example, you could add a night in the backcountry, seeing some of the sights less seen. You might decide to stay in one of the regions a day longer to work your hikes around the schedule and pace of the ranger-led hikes or to experience some far-flung area by horseback. The Many Glacier Region offers bountiful opportunities for horseback adventures, which children love. You might choose to add a second day in Lake McDonald for a horseback ride there. Maybe you will take an extra day in Two Medicine to rent kayaks for the family to paddle around the lake.

You can also extend your regional stays by adding additional hikes or hiking farther on any of the other trails we include in the shorter itineraries.

ADDING ADVENTURE TO YOUR TRIP

We've said it before but it bears repeating, Glacier is a particularly great park to drive through, but driving is never the best way for kids to enjoy a park, and it won't create the deep connection that our kids need to have with America's national parks in order to preserve them long into the future. Fortunately, there are many other wonderful ways to add adventure and motivate your kids. As a parent, you probably realize that the more connected they are to their surroundings, the easier it will be for you to enjoy yourself too! Read on for ways to add adventure to your Glacier trip, creating lasting memories for your family.

Hiking

Hiking is the cheapest and easiest way to infuse adventure into your visit. Walking is just the speed for kids to relish and appreciate nature. In this book you will find trail descriptions, written with your kids' enjoyment in mind, for all the main areas of the park;

Ranger-led hikes help you to appreciate the trail even more. (NPS/Jacob W. Frank photo)

CAUTION! ALPINE PLANTS

One thing to remember when hiking in the subalpine and alpine elevations near and above tree line in Glacier National Park is that the native soils and plants of this ecosystem are quite fragile. Growing seasons here are extremely short, so it can take plants decades to recover from damage caused by careless hikers; soil erosion takes even longer to repair. This is why the most popular trail at Logan Pass is mostly covered with boardwalk—to protect the native soils and plants. You can do your part when hiking in these areas by staying on existing trails where the dirt has already been compacted, and by stepping on rock or stone where possible and always trying to avoid stepping on the vegetation. We know it can be difficult to keep adventurous kids from straying off the trail. We find that taking some time to educate our kids on the reasons for the rules and inviting them to be conservationists and park protectors with us goes a long way toward keeping them on the designated trails.

Stay on the boardwalk to protect fragile alpine tundra.

Kayaking is one way to enjoy the many lakes of Glacier National Park.
(NPS/Jacob W. Frank photo)

these will help you plan an itinerary that works for each member of your family. Even if it is your first time hiking with the kids, or hiking in Glacier, you will feel confident about setting out on the trail because of the pertinent information you will find here.

Bicycling

Most kids love to ride a bicycle. We regularly see cars loaded up for vacation with a rack full of kids' bikes on the back. While bicycling is normally a great way to get kids into the outdoors, in Glacier National Park there are limited options for cycling. Much of Glacier is designated wilderness, and bikes aren't allowed in wilderness, so keep in mind that bikes are *not* allowed on trails unless it's specifically stated that they are (there are only three, each mentioned in the descriptions to follow). The narrow-shouldered roads are dangerous to ride on, with drivers so distracted by the scenery that they may fail to pay close enough attention to cyclists on the road. Campgrounds will be your best bet for letting the kids get out on their bikes.

Horseback Riding

Older, confident children will enjoy seeing the park on horseback. Horses can take you farther away from "civilization" than you can travel on foot. The park looks different from the back of a horse. If you are not a regular horseback rider, there are less pleasant consequences, including chafing and sore muscles and joints for one to two days afterward. You probably shouldn't plan on doing a long hike the day after your long ride!

Swimming

Kids seem to have a special attraction to water, and they will enjoy a hike more if there is some kind of water involved—be it creek, river, waterfall, or lake. While Glacier National Park's bodies of water are often too cold for full-body immersion, there are plenty of opportunities for a little splashing or wading. For particularly brave souls—and bodies—swimming is an option.

Boating

Whether you want to paddle your own canoe or take advantage of a guided boat tour on a historic wooden boat, you have plenty of opportunities to get on the water at Glacier; just be aware of some restrictions. You can usually bring your own personal watercraft to Glacier, but you need to get a (free) launch permit from one of the visitor centers, park headquarters, or a backcountry office before you launch. The permit is self-issue for all hand-propelled craft (rafts, kayaks, canoes, and stand-up paddleboards). For motorized watercraft, you will also need to get an inspection before a permit can be issued. Inspectors check for zebra mussels or other invasive species that might be hitching a ride; they also make sure that no oil, gas, or other fluids are leaking that might damage habitat.

At the time of this writing, in response to those invasive mussels, the park service has banned personal motorboats at Glacier but is allowing, in summer, hand-powered vessels as well as scenic boat tours. Make sure to check the Glacier National Park website for current information (see Resources) and boating regulations.

Bus Touring

There are various bus tour opportunities throughout much of Glacier National Park, and you may be tempted to give one or another of them a try. They can be great opportunities to see more of the park, without the hassle of driving yourself, and they can be educational. Before you sign up for any of them, however, survey your group. Families differ and while some will enjoy learning about and seeing the park from a bus seat, many kids may find it boring after a while, despite the cool features of some of the buses. While our family favored using the park service shuttle system for our "tours," your family may have different priorities. Consider your options:

Park service shuttle system: The free shuttle bus makes regular stops up and down Going-to-the-Sun Road throughout the day. Find maps and schedules at any visitor center, in the

An iconic Glacier National Park Red Bus

park newspaper, and online at the park's website. Although the free shuttle isn't billed as a "tour," the drivers are often entertaining and full of information about the park. If they don't offer history and science lessons on their own, just start asking questions. Many operators have been driving here for years and love to share all that they have learned.

Red Buses: The most iconic of the bus tours are the Red Buses run by Glacier National Park Lodges (see Resources). The vintage 1930s buses are now more reliable and "greener" than ever, updated to modern emissions standards to maintain the clean air in the park and revamped inside to give visitors the best views possible (very cool "roll back" tops show off the high peaks!). There are east and west side tours with multiple options on both sides of the park. The vehicles are interesting and your kid may think they want to take a ride, but keep in mind that the tours are long by children's standards, with little to do other than look out the window. Most kids will tire of this quickly. Tours range from three to four hours to up to eight hours. That's a lot of sitting for a kiddo! Consider skipping the tour and instead snap a selfie with the kids and one of these beautiful buses by heading over to the Lake McDonald Lodge where off-duty buses are parked; sometimes that's enough.

Sun Tours: These buses are roomy and comfortably seat from thirteen to twenty-five passengers. A bonus of Sun Tours is that little kids, five and under, ride free. They are led by guides from the Blackfeet Indian Reservation, who will share with you park history, information about common plant and animal species, and the Blackfeet spiritual and philosophical stories from life in the Buffalo Days and into modern times. While interesting to most adults (and some children), remember that a coach tour represents hours of sitting and listening; it's quite possible that your kids were hoping to avoid that during their vacation from school.

STEPS FOR PLANNING YOUR GLACIER FAMILY VACATION

The following is the tried and tested sequence we follow when planning our family park trips.

First, go to the maps section on the Glacier National Park website (see Resources), where you can download and print a park map or ask for it to be sent by mail. They will usually do this for free. It helps to have this big fold-out map next to you as you plan. We write all over ours as we make decisions, and it becomes a major part of the trip planning.

We also find it helpful to "like" the park's Facebook page. This keeps us informed on closures, schedules, activities, and more. With these tools to hand—and websites bookmarked—you are now ready to start the hardcore planning!

We recommend sights and adventures grouped by region: the west side's Lake McDonald, and the east side's St. Mary and Logan Pass, Many Glacier, and Two Medicine. Due to its remoteness, we have omitted the North Fork and Goat Haunt region. Decide what sights and attractions in Glacier you simply must see in order to feel like you got the most out of your visit. The Best Bets section will help with this, but you also might want to talk to friends or search the web to get other opinions. So often when our friends hear that we are planning a trip they will say, "Oh, you must see 'X'!" or "Don't miss 'Y'!" As you follow the next steps, keep track of which regions the things on your "to do" list are found in, as this will ease your planning immensely. As you organize your favorites, you may find that you don't need to visit every region in order to feel you've seen everything you want.

At the same time, you will likely need to think about how much time you have for your vacation. Refer back to our section on suggested itineraries for stays of various lengths. Usually you can find one that is close to what you are planning and then customize it for your personal situation.

Decide how much adventure you want to add to your trip. There are dozens of options for hiking, but there are also a few options for horseback rides, backpacking, boating, bicycling, bus touring, or even rafting (just outside the park). We have provided all the information you need to choose and book these adventures and have organized this information by region in our chapters and in the Resources section. Each of these adventures is evaluated and described with kids in mind.

Once you know which things you want to do, organize your information based on region, decide how much time you can spend per region, and then make your lodging choices accordingly. Most regions of the park have both camping and indoor lodging options, so you never have to stay too far from the action. However, many of the options that can be reserved in advance fill up as soon as they become available. Make sure to do your planning as much as six to seven months in advance if you can. The Glacier Camping and Lodging chapter will tell you what you need to know.

Now all that is left is to figure out how you are going to get there. There are many options, depending on where you live, but it basically comes down to driving in your own vehicle, flying to a nearby airport and then renting a car, or some combination of these that might include renting a recreational vehicle (RV). Each of these options has implications for how you will approach the question of where you will stay as well, so review Getting There earlier in this chapter.

If you plan to do any hiking at all, we also recommend purchasing the small packet of trail maps. These small fold-out maps for each of the four main regions offer more detailed information on the main hiking routes. You can purchase them at any of Glacier's ranger stations once you arrive.

There you go! We have always found that planning the trip is a big part of the fun of doing the trip; so read on and get started dreaming about your Glacier vacation!

Pick up handy hike maps at any of Glacier National Park's ranger stations.

Snow lasts throughout the summer at higher elevations.

BEST BETS

If you take the time and effort to journey across the country to Glacier National Park, there are a few things that you really owe it to yourself to see in order to get the most out of your experience. Below, we've sorted each feature by region to make your planning easier. We suggest you read through these, choose the ones you want to add to your own top activities list, and then read the detailed descriptions in the next chapter to make sure they are truly a good fit for your family or group.

The Glacier National Park map in this section provides an overview showing the regions of the park. More detailed maps of each region, which include hiking trails, distances, campsites, and more, can be found in the regional chapters.

The bowl for Avalanche Lake was carved out by ancient glaciers.

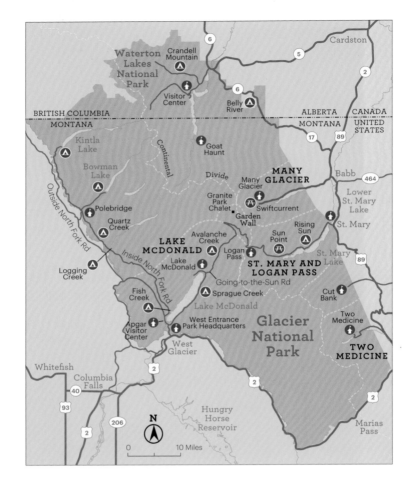

LAKE MCDONALD REGION

Everyone in our family loved the hike to Avalanche Lake. We highly recommend this hike, as it will give you a taste of the true flavor of Glacier National Park. It does involve a moderate change in elevation of 500 feet, but that is spread out over a reasonable distance. The other two hikes in Lake McDonald

The St. Mary and Logan Pass Region includes the "Garden Wall."

that made our favorites list are the Trail of the Cedars and the walk along McDonald Creek that is part of the Johns Lake Loop. Both are nearly level walks along beautiful trails.

Lake McDonald itself is also well worth seeing. Thanks to numerous pullouts and passes right along its southern shore, it can be readily viewed from Going-to-the-Sun Road.

ST. MARY AND LOGAN PASS REGION

The St. Mary Valley offers excellent waterfall hikes, with falls both big and small. In the Glacier Adventures by Region chapter, you will find short trails and longer loops that take in multiple falls. Our favorite hike is from Virginia Falls to St. Mary Falls, where many little falls along the way keep the trail from seeming too long or too hard. Each cascade is spectacular in its own way.

The National Park Service groups Logan Pass activities with those in St. Mary, so we do too. Many people—us included—take in the hikes on Logan Pass on a day trip from St. Mary; you can also access it from the Lake McDonald Region. The journey up to the pass, located at the very peak of Going-to-the-Sun Road, is stunning and can be done on a free shuttle, leaving your eyes free to take in all the sights. Even when all the wildflowers at lower elevations down have dried up and faded away, an amazing blanket of color is spread out around the Logan Pass Visitor Center.

We loved the beginning of the Highline Trail. Begin the trail from the Logan Pass Visitor Center, and walk as far as you are comfortable. Many of the best features (cliffsides, hanging gardens, and big views) come along the first part of the trail. Equally recommended is hiking to the Hidden Lake Overlook on a trail that takes you through an extensive alpine meadow. This is prime wildlife-viewing habitat, and many visitors have seen mountain goats and bighorn sheep up close here. You don't have to walk all the way to the lake to see these beautiful animals; the walk to the overlook is usually sufficient.

MANY GLACIER REGION

Many Glacier is a wonderful region to visit and offers countless hiking options. We very strongly recommend a trip to Redrock Falls, with a stop at Fishercap Lake to look for moose. The trail takes in typical terrain and views for this region—clear lakes, green forests, and sharp mountains rising above

The *Morning Eagle* carries hikers across Lake Josephine.

you—with the promise of a waterfall at the end. Our kids also loved the double boat ride option. It seemed adventurous to take the boat across Swiftcurrent Lake, get off and hike a short distance to Lake Josephine, and then hop on another boat. Having a destination made the ride high adventure and beat out the other tours that just loop around a lake. The shuttle across Josephine deposits you at the trailhead for both Grinnell Lake (an easy and beautiful hike) and Grinnell Glacier (a challenging but awe-inspiring hike). If you have the time and energy on your Glacier vacation for just one long, tough hike, the trail to Grinnell Glacier is the one to take. Also keep in mind that Grinnell Glacier is the most accessible glacier for you and the kids. You will be able to view other glaciers during your exploration of the park, but this is the only one we can generally recommend hiking to for most families.

TWO MEDICINE REGION

The Two Medicine area is a "must do" for families with kids (and even those without!) that want to hike. It is a bit more secluded and lacks the crowds found in many other areas of the park. We suggest first taking the short stroll to Running Eagle/Trick Falls on the drive in. The falls are a wonder of nature, and the trail is accessible to anyone, so check it out! We also loved hiking to Aster Falls and relaxing there. For the most adventurous families, Rockwell Falls is an absolute must do, offering hours of exploring, climbing, foot soaking, and relaxing. And if you are up for taking a 45-minute boat ride the length of Two Medicine Lake, do it: from the end of the ride, it is only two more relatively flat hiking miles to reach Upper Two Medicine Lake, an excellent picnic spot if the weather cooperates.

WILDLIFE VIEWING

Glacier has many dazzling places to visit, and a big part of their beauty is that they represent natural, large-scale, unspoiled habitat of a type that we don't often experience—the mid- and upper alpine. Glacier National Park is home to 71 different species of mammals, including lynx and wolverine, animals that are quite rare in the Lower 48, and more than 275 species of birds spend some part of the year here. This chapter will give you some good ideas on where to get started in your quest for wildlife, and which critters you are most likely to see.

Keep in mind that the majority of animals are most active during the earliest and latest parts of the day. For the best chance of seeing them, make the effort to get up early and head out at first light to some of the areas we mention. Likewise, consider having an early dinner and then spending the waning hours of daylight in the field, which dramatically improves your odds of seeing something. Finally, it never hurts to bring along a few pairs of binoculars. We find that giving our kids their own binoculars, and even their own cameras, increases their enjoyment and the amount of time they will tolerate sitting around looking for wildlife. The national park warns about getting too close to wild animals and, in fact, gives specific minimum distances to remain from the park's wildlife; know and follow these guidelines! Animals may seem "friendly," but this is not a petting zoo. They are focused primarily on survival, and from a human standpoint they are unpredictable, so maintain a safe distance. And never feed any of the animals.

Mountain Goats

Mountain goats are some of the more unusual mammals in North America, but fortunately they are very common in Glacier, so much so that they are essentially the park's mascot. These fascinating animals have a two-layer coat that enables them to withstand temperatures of –50 degrees F and winds up to 100 mph. They also have unique hooves that feature a hard outer shell but a softer inner pad that allows them to grip rock surfaces very effectively.

Just about anywhere that you find steep rocky cliffs above tree line, there is the possibility of seeing a goat, but by far the easiest place to view them is at Logan Pass. They can often be

Odds are you'll spot a few mountain goats in the park.

on the steep slopes near the first bend of Going-to-the-Sun just west of the pass. But if you really want the best chance to view them and get some great pictures, hike the boardwalk trail out to the Hidden Lake Overlook; it is prime goat habitat. Another reliable area to see mountain goats is the early section of the Oberlin Mountain climbers route. Both hikes are covered in our St. Mary and Logan Pass section.

Bighorn Sheep

While mountain goats tend to favor the very highest reaches of the mountains and the sheerest of cliff faces, bighorn sheep like it just one step down, and it's not uncommon to find the two in close proximity. Logan Pass is a great place to see bighorn sheep, and there is a resident herd that lives in the immediate area. These native sheep favor steep, grassy slopes with rough, rocky terrain close by to use for escape and taking cover from predators.

Another excellent location to spot bighorn sheep is along the Grinnell Glacier trail in the Many Glacier Region; they are very common along the middle and upper sections of the trail, for

Keep your eyes peeled in early morning and late afternoon to spot bighorn sheep, like this impressive ram.

those with the stamina to get that far. In the Two Medicine area, we have seen bighorns right around Appistoki Falls and, especially, in the sweeping alpine bowls beyond these falls along the trail that leads to Scenic Overlook.

Bighorns are not as ubiquitous as mountain goats at Glacier, and because they don't wear coats of brilliant white hair, they are comparatively harder to see. It helps to remember that goats tend to be around most of the day, whereas bighorn sheep are active in the early and later hours of the day. Mornings and early evenings are the times you'll want to be out looking for bighorn sheep.

Moose

These massive beasts are the largest members of the deer family. You'll most often spot them in or near water, due to their size, insulating hollow hair (which makes them susceptible to overheating), and diet preferences. When the weather rises above a mere 60 degrees F, moose seek out the water to keep cool, and during the summer months their favorite foods are the succulent plants that grow on lake and river bottoms. When moose aren't in the water, they tend to prefer the cool shade of older forests. We have most often encountered them in marshy areas and along streams. The best bet for viewing moose in the Two Medicine area is the marshy ponds less than a mile from the trailhead on the Aster Falls Trail.

In the Many Glacier Region, you are most likely to see moose along the Swiftcurrent Pass Trail. The first lake you come to along this trail is shallow Fishercap Lake, where abundant sun reaches the bottom of the lake encouraging the growth of the food that the moose enjoy. Just 3 miles farther along this mellow trail takes you to Bullhead Lake. You can guess by the name that this is a well-known location for moose. The challenge is that they may well be gone by the time you arrive; to avoid the heat, moose are typically active only early and late in the day.

Another likely moose spot is along the shores of Swiftcurrent Lake. We have seen moose here during boat tours, and we have

We saw this moose in the Many Glacier Region.

seen them at the inlet stream from Lake Josephine while hiking the lake's nature trail. If you travel to the far end of Lake Josephine to hike into Grinnell Glacier, you'll want to know that the river bottom areas of the Grinnell Lake drainage are also excellent moose habitat.

Bears

An estimated 300 grizzly bears and 600 black bears live in Glacier National Park, so learning about bear behavior and how to travel safely in bear country is extremely important. Make sure you and your family know how to stay safe and avoid any close encounters with these magnificent animals. Grizzlies tend to live higher up in the mountains and prefer the alpine areas in the summer, whereas black bears frequent the lower, forested areas. Most of the black bears our family has seen in the park have been along the road early in the morning while we were driving to a trailhead or when trying to snag an open campsite before the sites filled up. Our closest grizzly encounter was

Use your zoom lens for grizzlies!

right up near the Continental Divide in Granite Park. After we had hiked to the chalet, Harley continued along the Highline Trail toward the Grinnell Glacier Overlook. As he came around a bend he saw an enormous sow digging for ground squirrels along the trail. The tremendous strength she demonstrated as she flung earth with her huge front quarters was humbling and a bit terrifying. After Harley waited about fifteen minutes for her to move along so he could continue down the trail, she finally gathered her yearling cub and ambled off.

Another great place to spot grizzlies is from the porch or parking lot around the Many Glacier Hotel, with views of the ridge of mountains north of the Many Glacier entrance road from Apikuni Falls all the way to Altyn Peak. It is very common to see people in this area looking through binoculars and scopes to view the awesome creatures from a distance.

Learn more about how to stay safe hiking and recreating in bear country in the Safety in the Park chapter, and on the Glacier National Park website (see Resources).

Deer

Two varieties of deer are found in the park, whitetail deer and mule deer, the latter so named because of their huge, antennae-like ears

Male whitetail deer with antlers in velvet (NPS/Jon Riner photo)

reminiscent of a mule. Mule deer also have a black tail (but are not black-tailed deer!). While mule deer tend to favor more open habitat further up the mountain, whitetails like to browse and rest in heavier forest. But in truth, you can encounter either of these species almost anywhere in the park, making it difficult for us to single out a place to recommend. Still, as long as you get out and hike a number of trails, chances are good you will see deer, always a wonderful family experience.

Elk

The magnificent elk is another iconic deer species found in Glacier. A big cousin to whitetail and mule deer, elk live in almost every region of the park yet are seldom encountered by park visitors. The one place where you are most likely to find them is Two Dog Flats, between the St. Mary Visitor Center and the

Elk are another animal most often seen early or late in the day.

Rising Sun Campground. This open meadow provides excellent browse for elk and is ringed by aspen trees and mixed forest, another habitat type favored by these animals. Elk are always looking for the greenest grass they can find. The newest growth provides the best nutrition and is easiest to digest, so in the spring elk follow the snow line as it recedes up the mountain to forage on the emerging grasses on newly exposed and damp soils. Having a pair of binoculars to scan the edges of meadows early and late in the day increases your chances of seeing elk. We've also been fortunate enough to catch them grazing on the shoulder of Going-to-the-Sun Road. Such is the unpredictable nature of wildlife observation!

Wolverines

Glacier National Park holds the largest density of wolverines in the Lower 48, so you might think that your chances of seeing one are good. Sadly, "largest" still means only fifty total of these amazing critters in the park, and wolverines are highly nomadic, traveling large distances in search of food. Wolverines are also extremely wary; they seem to never walk anywhere, only run. The upshot is that they are unlikely to be where you are.

Wolverines are fierce and expert scavengers, and the majority of their diet is carrion from the carcasses of large mammals like deer and elk. But they are also excellent hunters of smaller mammals such as snowshoe hares, marmots, and squirrels. The largest member of the weasel family, wolverines tend to favor stands of subalpine fir with deep snow cover. In spring they den in snow, and they frequent snow slides to search for mountain

goats and bighorn sheep that were buried by snow or avalanche during the winter. Because wolverines are also very dark and stand out against the snow, they are sometimes spotted during the early visitor season in the Logan Pass area and along the Highline Trail. If you are lucky enough to spot one of these animals, you should count yourself fortunate indeed.

If you happen to spot a wolverine, like this one near the Grinnell Glacier, count yourself very fortunate indeed. (Erik Peterson photo)

Other Predators

Glacier National Park supports healthy populations of mountain lions, lynx, wolves, coyotes, and foxes, but your chances of actually spotting any of these animals are very low. Mountain lions have huge home ranges; they are also crepuscular (in action during the early evening hours) and secretive, making sightings extremely rare. Lynx prefer dense stands of timber where they pursue their favorite prey, the snowshoe hare. Wolves are also nomadic and shy, so they are more likely to be heard than seen. Their howls carry long distances, and your family may indeed *hear* wolves in the park. The seldom-visited northwest portion of the park holds the largest numbers of wolves, but it is also heavily forested and has relatively few access points and resources, so we don't really recommend it as a place to take the family. Foxes are a bit more common, as are coyotes, but there is really no surefire strategy for spotting them. Encounters with these amazing animals are more likely to be a product of serendipity than of planning.

To stay safe, in the event that you do encounter a mountain lion, stay in a group with children near parents. Don't run; rather, stand tall and make noise, giving it a chance to leave. Finally, if it becomes aggressive, throw sticks or stones at it while continuing to make a lot of noise.

A NOTE ABOUT SAFETY

Glacier is fundamentally a wild place. While that is one of its greatest attractions, it also carries with it certain risks. We have done our best to provide reasonable advice and guidance on how to have a fun, safe, adventurous family vacation in the park, but there is no way that we can write a book that is a substitute for the reader's sound judgment. Conditions in the mountains change quickly, and only you can respond to those changes; a book cannot. Every family is made up of members with differing strengths and weaknesses. You know your family, and we do not. So, do your research and make your plans, and then make the right decisions when you are in the park and faced with your specific circumstances. We are confident that with the right preparation and planning you will have a safe and excellent vacation, but we cannot *guarantee* that outcome.

The glacial waters of McDonald Creek are beautiful but very cold.

GLACIER ADVENTURES BY REGION

We begin each regional adventure section with what most people come to Glacier to do: hike. Our hike descriptions are tailored to traveling and hiking with kids, with particular attention paid to what makes the hike fun for them, as well as the adults in the party. Following the hiking options, we include other enjoyable ways to add adventure to your trip, including boating, horseback riding, biking, and more. As you read through the various options, keep track of the ones that sound the most exciting for your family. Remember that a memorable national park vacation doesn't mean you did everything, only that each member of your family or group found something that captured their imagination and brought them inspiration.

LAKE MCDONALD REGION

The Lake McDonald Region is found on the west side of Glacier National Park and is characterized by activities surrounding the lake or hikes up into the mountains that flank the lake on all sides. This area is also the hub of nearly all activity on its side of the park. There are ranger stations and small campgrounds scattered all along the western border of the park, but the main hiking trails and activities are concentrated in the area around the lake.

At 10 miles long and 500 feet deep, Lake McDonald is the largest lake in Glacier National Park. It was carved by glacial action, the evidence of which is seen all over the park. If you want to learn more about how glaciers have been at work in this area, take the time to hike along with a ranger or attend a naturalist's program. They'll likely share information with you that will feel especially relevant when you are later staring nature in the eye.

Things You Need to Know

Glacier National Park has three visitor centers. Apgar Visitor Center is located at the southwestern end of Lake McDonald near the west entrance of the park, and it's where you'll find alerts for road and trail closures, weather warnings, and other

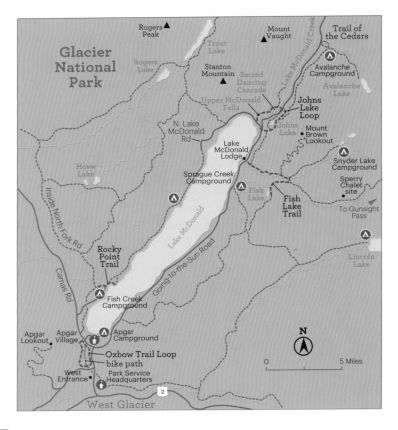

Taking the Junior Ranger Oath is a bit of a thrill for kids. (NPS/Jacob W. Frank photo)

pertinent and up-to-date information for the western portion of the park. At Apgar you can also check on the status of campground openings for the first-come, first-served campgrounds (see Glacier Camping and Lodging). As mentioned in the Top Five Tips section, for most kids it is better to get out and onto the trails than to spend too much time in a visitor center. Make your "check-in" short and sweet and then get out on the trails.

Apgar Visitor Center is a smaller office than many that we have visited. It is staffed with knowledgeable rangers but doesn't offer much more than that. Get in line to talk with a ranger and then make sure to ask for a park map, a ranger-led activity guide, and the park newspaper; each offers insights into research and the history of the park. While you are there, be sure to sign your kids up for the Junior Ranger program, in which your kids can earn a ranger badge for completing some fun required activities. The program is free to you and, besides providing hours of entertainment, gives them tangibles to focus on while you are out exploring.

One final item: The park offers a free shuttle to many of the main hiking locations, a great option that saves you gas, frees up time otherwise spent waiting for parking spots, and minimizes congestion and pollution in the park. Check out the current schedule of times and stops. The Apgar Visitor Center is also the main hub for the shuttle on the west side of the park.

The following are some of the best loved and better known hikes, which we present based on our own experience. We will tell you what our kids loved—and what they wish we had skipped—to help you make an informed plan for how your family will spend time in this region of the park.

Hiking Adventures

 ### Johns Lake Loop

After hooking around Johns Lake and meandering through cedar forests, the Johns Lake Loop eventually meets up with the stunning McDonald Creek Trail. The entire trail may not appeal to all families, but you won't want to miss the section along McDonald Creek itself—it's a delight!

Distance: 3 miles with 160 feet of elevation gain
Time: 2–3 hours
Starting point: The hike begins and ends at the Johns Lake Loop trailhead parking pullout, which is small and so can be a bit tricky to locate. As you are heading east on Going-to-the-Sun Road, the pullout is on your right just before the left-hand turn for North Lake McDonald Road.

The loop can be hiked in either direction; however, it is easier to follow if you go in the counterclockwise direction and always choose the uphill option when you arrive at an intersection.

The trail winds gradually uphill through a cedar forest to Johns Lake. You will catch a first glimpse of the lake and be tempted to head over and check it out. Sure, you *can* do that,

There's not a lot of shoreline at Johns Lake, but the views are nice.

but if you continue on there is a better approach to the water just a bit farther on. Normally any water feature is a big positive when hiking with kids, but Johns Lake was a bit disappointing. Access to the lake is difficult. It is heavily surrounded by forest, the "beach front" is minimal at best, and the shoreline is boggy. There were no rocks to skip or leaves to sail as boats. The kids found playing on rocks and old logs to be a much more attractive prospect than swimming or wading in the actual lake.

After leaving Johns Lake, the trail heads downward back toward the road. When you reach the road, you will need to cautiously cross it to reach the parking area, heading left to see McDonald Creek and its bridge. There are stairs down to the bridge and also down to the creek itself. This beautiful spot is a welcome place to take a snack break and let the kids throw some rocks. You'll want to pay special attention to your children along this creek, because the water is both cold and swift. The number one cause of fatalities in Glacier National Park is actually water hazards (not grizzly bears!), so vigilance around streams is always advised.

You could stay on the near side of the creek and continue downstream if you so desire, but we recommend you continue

by crossing the bridge and turning left to follow the
downstream. This far-side trail is high above the creek
rs beautiful views back upstream and down onto a
series of falls, whereas the near-side trail hangs too
close to the road. Your children will enjoy the wide trail through
trees near the creek, but continue to keep them close to you.

Finally, the trail bends away from the creek to return to
a service road. Along this part of the trail, as you cross a car
bridge, you will encounter views down into Lake McDonald
itself. To finish the loop, hike along the road or on the roadside
trail until you reach the main road, across from the parking
area. Cross to your car with care.

While we do not feel we can recommend this *entire* hike to
all families with kids (who may be bored on the portion of the
hike to the east of Going-to-the-Sun Road), we loved the part of
the trail along McDonald Creek and highly recommend that. If
you want a shorter option that gets you to the best part of the
hike first, then park your car at the large pullout on the south-
east side of the main road near the crossing bridge and quickly
reach the part of the hike that is most interesting. If you hike
only this section, you will retrace your steps along the creek to
return to your car.

 Trail of the Cedars Boardwalk

People of all ages will be awed and enchanted by this loop walk
on a boardwalk through old-growth cedar groves. The trail is
wheelchair accessible.

Distance: 0.7-mile loop with no elevation gain
Time: 30–45 minutes
Starting point: Trail of the Cedars trailhead along Going-to-the-Sun
Road near the Avalanche Campground

To hike this wonderful boardwalk loop through old cedar
groves, stay to the left at the branch that leads to Avalanche

There's a reason they call it the "trail of the cedars."

Lake. Wander along at your family's pace, enjoying the trees and glimpses of Avalanche Creek flowing through the forest around you. This is a shady trail, so best to save it for the hottest part of the day. The hike is so easy that we didn't plan on doing it; but if we hadn't, boy, would we have missed out. It is so short and easy that everyone can do it and all will enjoy it!

 Avalanche Lake

This moderate hike is well worth the time and effort it requires, as it shows off sights unique to Glacier National Park, from glacier-carved turquoise lakes to high waterfalls to lush forests. Try to join a ranger-led hike to learn about how the terrain became what it is today.

Distance: 3.8 miles with 500 feet of elevation gain
Time: 3–4 hours
Starting point: Trail of the Cedars trailhead: look for the Avalanche Gorge Bridge along Going-to-the-Sun Road.

This trail is one of the only family-friendly hikes in the Lake McDonald Region that truly gives you a taste of the essence of Glacier National Park, and it is one you won't want to miss. When we hiked this trail and reached Avalanche Lake, we knew we were someplace very special! Here you will see obvious evidence of glaciation and avalanches. To learn much more about the rocks, rivers, lakes, and avalanche and glaciation history in Glacier, try to coordinate your schedule with a ranger-led hike. We would have walked past so many interesting phenomena if we had hiked the trail on our own. The ranger is your guide and storyteller going up, but after reaching the top you're on your own to retrace your steps back to the trailhead. This worked well for us since our kids craved that opportunity to be independent and explore for themselves.

The trail starts along the Trail of the Cedars loop, but you soon come to an intersection with your trail, the main Avalanche

A log jam obscures Avalanche Lake's turquoise water, but there is better access ahead.

Lake Trail. Continue up the trail as it follows an enchanting, river-filled gorge. The rock here was carved by ancient ice into loops and whorls, and the gorge was steep and narrow. The trail gives you plenty of room, which helps relieve your worries about the kids approaching the edge, but do keep an eye on them as your family explores around the gorge itself.

Eventually the trail leaves the gorge and enters forest. Evidence of avalanches is everywhere, although the signs can be misinterpreted or missed altogether without a ranger as your guide. The terrain here is rolling, and the trail climbs and falls over mounds and humps: steep in places and breathless going, but if you are with a ranger they will give you plenty of opportunities to rest along the way! (If you're on your own, just keep track of how everyone is feeling and take breaks as they are needed.) Be sure to stop at the wide opening to the left side of the trail in this forested section, for views up to Hidden Creek and the Hidden Lake Trail dropping off the top of Logan Pass. Look also for wildlife: bears are often sighted on the hillside across the valley from where you stand.

Next, the trail breaks out of the older forest into smaller trees and more open terrain, indicating that you're getting close to the lake.

Soon you will see a large logjam formed at the base of the lake. You can leave the trail at this point and walk down to get your first lake views and to take photos. Don't get too comfortable here though, as a better place for stopping with a much larger, rocky sand beach awaits just around the corner. Follow the trail through more brushy areas, past a group of pit toilet bathrooms, and over a boardwalk to the main beach.

Large rocks and driftwood logs on the beach provide a rest spot for a satisfying break. The trail continues around the lake, but this is the final destination for most people. Enjoy your stay for as long as you like before heading back the way you came.

 Rocky Point

The Rocky Point Trail leads through a variety of terrain as it winds along the western shore of Lake McDonald, eventually turning uphill to gain views from a higher elevation. Keep the kids engaged by asking them if they can spot evidence of fires from the recent past.

Distance: 2.2 miles in a lollipop loop, 85 feet of elevation gain
Time: 1–2 hours
Starting point: To reach the trailhead, from its intersection with Going-to-the-Sun Road, drive 1.2 miles north on Camas Road. Turn right onto Fish Creek Campground Road, and drive another 1.1 miles to the campground entrance. From here turn left onto gravel Inside North Fork Road, and drive 0.4 mile to the parking area for the Rocky Point Trail on the left side of the road. The Rocky Point trailhead is located across the road from the parking area.

Before setting out on this hike, you should know that there are numbered benches along the way that correspond to a park service publication that enlightens visitors on the role fire plays in forest habitats. Ask at the Apgar Visitor Center for the Rocky Point Nature Trail Guide, or find it at the Glacier National Park website (see Resources).

Campers staying at the Fish Creek Campground can depart directly from the campground, heading east when they reach the trail, or drive to the nearby trailhead. If entering the trail from the North Fork Road trailhead, you will encounter the campground trail entering from the right, so stay to the left. The trail begins as a mostly level meander through grasses, flowers, and occasional coniferous trees.

The forest deepens, and at 0.6 mile you come to the "loop" part of the "lollipop loop." To reach the lake soonest and have the most gradual elevation gain, take the right branch. All along this part of the trail you will see glimpses of the lake. Shortly after starting on the loop, you come to another branch that eventually leads down to Lake McDonald but also reaches the

You get peek-a-boo views of distant peaks beyond Lake McDonald on the Rocky Point Trail.

Rocky Point viewpoint. Enjoy the views before retracing your steps to the main trail.

Continue around the lake until the trail turns to head uphill. You will begin to see the massive damage caused by the 2003 fires that burned in this part of the park. As the trail reaches the high point, you will get more views of the lake from a new perspective.

At 1.2 miles, reach a junction with the Lake McDonald Trail. Take the left-hand trail to finish the loop and head back to the trailhead on the section you walked in on.

 Oxbow Trail

A lovely meander through the forest along the shore of McDonald Creek as it exits Lake McDonald, this trail provides views of beaver dams—and a chance to appreciate how industrious animals can affect the flow of waterways.

Distance: 1 mile with little to no elevation gain
Time: 1–2 hours
Starting point: South side of the McDonald Creek Bridge on Camas Road, to the west of Apgar Visitor Center

---

The hike begins immediately south of Camas Road where it crosses McDonald Creek leaving Lake McDonald. You will begin by heading down the trail toward the creek and then along its banks. Soon the trail bends inland, and you leave the creek for a bit. The trail meanders among brush, grasses, and trees making for a mostly shady hike that takes you to various overlook points along the river, including one where some industrious beavers have built a dam and the river oxbows, becoming wide and slow. Beavers are considered the great engineers of natural waterways for good reason!

After the beaver dam overlook, the trail winds back into deeper forest, where you are presented with some trail options. Try to avoid the rutted horse-trail section, which is unpleasant and hard for little ones to walk on. Eventually all the trails meet up with the paved path that connects back to the parking area, completing the loop.

Overall, this trail is easy and pleasant. Its main interest for kids lies in the beaver dam and beaver folk who created the hike's namesake. Due to the height of the trail above the river, the water in the creek is accessible for wading or foot soaking only at the very beginning.

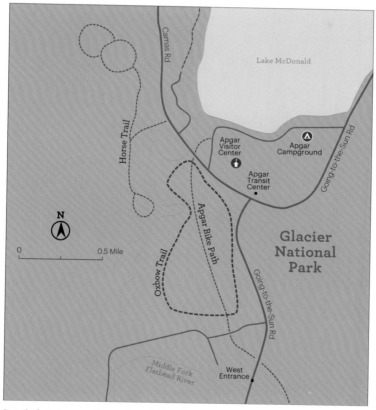

Detail of area around the Oxbow Trail and Apgar Bike Path

Evening is a great time to hike the Oxbow Trail.

Fish Lake is serenely beautiful.

 Fish Lake Trail

A steep and rigorous hike through old-growth forests to a high mountain lake, the trail to Fish Lake isn't for everyone, but it offers a challenge for ambitious young hikers.

Distance: 5.8 miles round-trip, with an elevation gain of 1210 feet
Time: 3–5 hours
Starting point: Sperry Trailhead, across the main street from the Lake McDonald Lodge turnoff from Going-to-the-Sun Road

---

The hike begins at the Sperry trailhead and branches many times, each branch but one, a horse path, being well marked. For a smoother trail, we recommend staying to the main trail and avoiding any obvious horse paths.

You immediately begin to knock off the elevation, climbing steeply up and away from Lake McDonald until you reach the Mount Brown Trail junction, about 1.6 miles in. At this point you have already climbed 900 feet above the trailhead! Although steep, the trail in this section leads through beautiful old-growth forest with views back to Lake McDonald, and a good chance of seeing deer. Don't forget to enjoy both as you struggle onward and upward.

Shortly past the Mount Brown Trail junction, you reach a left-branching trail to Snyder Lake. Keep right instead, and enjoy a short downhill cruise to the Snyder Creek Bridge crossing. Don't forget that bridges are magic for kids! Tossing leaves and sticks off the upstream side and running to see them pass under and downstream is an ageless pastime. Beyond the bridge is the junction with the Snyder Ridge Trail, which leads to Fish Lake. Take this right-hand branch and begin to climb up again.

The way is steep again but much shorter this time. As you reach the top you are rewarded with a long, mostly level trail that crosses the river a few more times before leading you to the shores of Fish Lake. Appreciate the levelness and the mossy forest.

The lake is below you as you come upon it. This is the best access point; scramble down to the banks to enjoy a hard-earned, refreshing break. The edges of the lake are largely covered in lily pads, but where the water is visible, it is amazingly clear. Linger to enjoy a rest and refueling stop, then head back the way you came.

This hike is steep and will be a real challenge for most kids. We did it with kids aged ten to fourteen (with a three-year-old in a backpack) and they all made it, but they didn't have much fun on the hiking part for sure. Also, the "fun" factor of being near water was diminished by the fact that there is hardly any beach area, no rocks to throw, and no real swim or splash opportunities. On the other hand, the forest you travel through along the trail, while not that different from what you might see in some other parts of the northern United States and Canada, is pretty impressive, and some kids will appreciate the chance to test themselves with a bit of elevation gain, even if the ultimate destination isn't as exciting as some others.

Adventures Beyond Hiking

Although hiking may be the first thing that comes to mind when you think of a trip to a national park, we want to challenge you to think outside that particular box. There are a few other options that are particularly great in this part of the park, as well as some that might sound like a good idea but that we think you'd do better to skip. Read on!

Boating

The west side of Glacier National Park is close to the Middle and North Forks of the Flathead River, which are protected as part of America's National Wild and Scenic Rivers System.

Who *doesn't* enjoy a boat ride?

There are four rafting companies that have contracts with the park service to provide whitewater rafting experiences. You can choose from half-day to all-day options, our favorite being the "saddle-paddle," which gives you a taste of whitewater followed by horseback riding! For traditional raft trips, check out the commercial guides listed on the park's website (or in Resources).

While you might think that a boat ride on Lake McDonald sounds good, consider whether your kids are the sort to enjoy a fairly passive experience. The staff is friendly and helpful, and the atmosphere on the boat dock is one of relaxed competence, but this particular boat tour is not one we recommend for younger kids. It is slow, and to a child much of the scenery looks the same. Enjoy this region on foot instead, saving your money for boat rides in other portions of the park that lead you to exciting trailheads and save you miles of walking! If there are adults or older kids in your group who want to go on the tour, however, there is a nice rocky beach with a stream near the boat dock where smaller children could play happily with a supervising adult while others in the group go on the boat ride. If you do decide to take a boat tour, advance reservations are highly recommended (and in some cases required); contact the Glacier Park Boat Company (see Resources).

Bus Touring

The free park shuttle, the Red Bus tours, and the Sun Tours all provide tours and access to the Lake McDonald region. The free shuttle bus travels along Going-to-the-Sun Road from Lake McDonald to the top of Logan Pass, with stops at major hiking and viewing attractions along the way. You can ride to the top and switch to a bus that will take you down the east side of the park if you wish to see the other side. Find more details on bus touring in the Planning Your Glacier Family Vacation chapter and check out Resources for contact information for reservations.

Bicycling

For the most part, this region of the park isn't suitable for kids to ride their bikes, but there are exceptions. We found some good mountain-bike riding on Inside North Fork Road to the west of Apgar near the Fish Creek Campground, as well as a nice, if short, bike path from the Apgar Visitor Center to the McDonald Creek Bridge. You'll probably want to keep your kids off Going-to-the-Sun Road, where they'd be sharing the surface with motor vehicles, but many kids enjoy some bike time in the campgrounds.

Horseback Riding

Swan Mountain Outfitters is the provider for all horseback rides in Glacier National Park (see Resources). They are a family-friendly outfitter committed to providing families with a great experience. They offer all sorts of horse-packing services (for backpackers and the chalets) but specialize in trail rides. In the Lake McDonald Region they offer rides from two different corral areas: Apgar and Lake McDonald. The Apgar corrals are just inside the main entrance near Apgar, and the Lake McDonald corrals are across from the Lake McDonald Lodge. They each offer a variety of rides ranging from one-hour to all-day rides. The terrain varies from mostly level terrain to steep, rugged terrain based on your ability level. As we said above, a great option for the very adventurous is the "saddle-paddle" option run by Swan Mountain, which allows you time to ride a horse and then a whitewater raft!

Fishing

Unfortunately, while all the water in Glacier makes for excellent habitat for many species of fish, the fishing opportunities for kids are somewhat limited. Most options are more appropriate for those with more experience, especially in fly-fishing. If you—or your kids—still want to try your luck, be sure to read all the guidelines at the park's website (see Resources), and talk to a ranger to be certain you are following current regulations before you fish.

Services and Amenities

The main entrance for the west side of the park, the Lake McDonald Region offers many services divided between two main locations: Apgar Village at the west end of the lake and Lake McDonald Lodge at the east end.

In the Apgar area, just beyond the Apgar Visitor Center are lodging, restaurants, the Discovery Cabin, a camp store, gift shops, some cell coverage, an ATM, church services, and water sport rentals. These are your closest services if you are staying at Fish Creek Campground, Apgar Village Lodge & Cabins, or Village Inn at Apgar.

The Lake McDonald Lodge area includes restaurants, a camp store, gift shops, an ATM, and religious services, as well as reservation counters for horseback riding, boating, and the Red Bus tours.

For better cell service, a post office, and gas stations, travel outside the park to the town of West Glacier. West Glacier also offers tour information for adventures in the areas surrounding the park.

ST. MARY AND LOGAN PASS REGION

Located on the east side of the park and situated as the main entrance for visitors arriving from the east, this area boasts the most resources and assistance in finalizing your plans for your visit. This region is known for waterfalls (St. Mary) and alpine habitat with wildlife (Logan Pass). A fire in 2015 burned the lower areas around the lake, greatly changing the experience for guests.

Things You Need to Know

As the main entrance for people arriving from the east, this area gets busy. Fortunately, there are multiple camping and lodging options to help accommodate the large number of visitors. There is also a free shuttle system for people wanting to visit

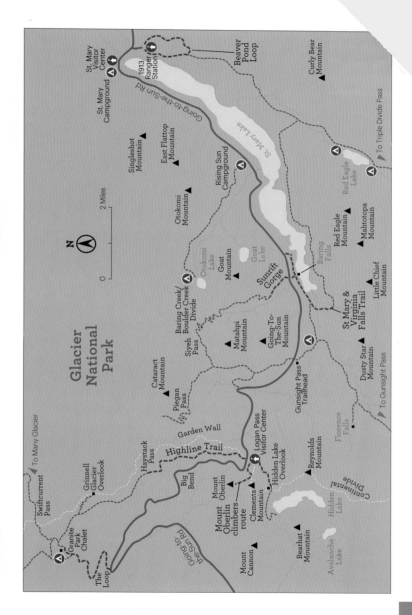

Glacier National Park

N

0   2 Miles

Swiftcurrent Pass

To Many Glacier

Grinnell Glacier Overlook

Granite Park Chalet

The Loop

Going-to-the-Sun Rd

Haystack Pass

Big Bend

Highline Trail

Garden Wall

Cataract Mountain

Piegan Pass

Siyeh Pass

Baring Creek/Boulder Creek Divide

Otokomi Mountain

Singleshot Mountain

East Flattop Mountain

St. Mary Campground

St. Mary Visitor Center

1913 Ranger Station

Beaver Pond Loop

Curly Bear Mountain

Going-To-The-Sun Rd

Rising Sun Campground

St. Mary Lake

To Triple Divide Pass

Red Eagle Lake

Otokomi Lake

Goat Lake

Goat Mountain

Matahpi Mountain

Going-To-The-Sun Mountain

Sunrift Gorge

Baring Falls

Red Eagle Mountain

Mahtotopa Mountain

Little Chief Mountain

St Mary & Virginia Falls Trail

Mount Oberlin

Mount Oberlin climbers route

Clements Mountain

Logan Pass Visitor Center

Hidden Lake Overlook

Gunsight Pass Trailhead

Dusty Star Mountain

To Gunsight Pass

Mount Cannon

Bearhat Mountain

Reynolds Mountain

Hidden Lake

Avalanche Lake

Continental Divide

Florence Falls

Going-to-the-Sun Rd

along Going-to-the-Sun Road. With its plethora of easy hikes, which can be joined together for those r something longer, the St. Mary area is good for all ability levels.

In 2015 an extensive forest fire burned much of the area immediately surrounding the lake, but don't decide against visiting because of that; there is beauty in regeneration. The undergrowth is springing up and presenting flowers throughout the summer season. The many colors of the flowers against the black of the burned trees are visually stunning. The fire burned branches, leaves, and needles, leaving a much less obscured view of the breathtaking mountains up the valley as you hike in that direction.

Although there are no places to overnight on Logan Pass, there is a visitor center and several hikes that families will enjoy. This part of the park can easily be sampled in a day trip from either the Lake McDonald or St. Mary region.

Hiking Adventures

 Beaver Pond Loop

Do you want an easy trail that offers solitude (and maybe animal sightings too)? Get away from many of the crowds in the St. Mary and Logan Pass Region on this short and sweet loop.

Distance: 3.3 miles for the full loop, with negligible elevation gain
Time: 0.5–1.5 hours
Starting point: Exit the St. Mary entrance station as if you were leaving the park (make sure you have your pass to get back in!), and take an immediate right where you see a large sign directing you to the historic 1913 ranger station. Follow this paved road for a short time, until it curves around to the left. At this curve, a gravel road heads off in the direction you are already driving. Take this gravel road a short distance to the parking area with bathroom that is situated on the valley floor below the old ranger station buildings.

A note about the distance and official trail: the maps and the signs give different distances for this trail. In fact, it is not even clear exactly which route is the official trail. Don't let this deter you! If you have come seeking time in the outdoors away from the crowds, you will find it here, regardless of whether you are on the "correct" trail.

Beginning on open level ground, the trail heads out into the valley area toward St. Mary Lake, passing through stands of aspen trees whose growth has been stunted by the winds that frequent this area. After about 15 to 20 minutes, you reach a boggy area to the left—old beaver ponds. Continue on to a split in the trail: the right-hand branch heads uphill into pine forest, while the left branch leads toward the lake. Choose the lakeshore path, where another split leads down onto the rocky beach. This is a great place for kids—and adults—to stop and play. Our kids would have thrown rocks there all day if we hadn't made them move on after half an hour! While you can return to the first split and head uphill into the forest, that route may seem a bit dull after the energy of the lakeshore, so it's best to return to your starting point after the lake.

The trail to Beaver Pond takes you by this beach on St. Mary Lake; it's perfect for skipping rocks.

A tiny waterfall awaits behind a hidden bend.

Sunrift Gorge

There's a delightful surprise at the end of this very short but sweet hike to a miniature gorge. It also shares a parking area with Baring Falls, so consider allowing enough time to do both hikes together.

Distance: 200 yards, with negligible elevation gain
Time: 10–15 minutes
Starting point: Sunrift Gorge parking area along Going-to-the-Sun Road. Take the free shuttle to get there, or park on either side of the road nearby.

A staircase from the south side of the road takes you under the highway so you don't have to cross it. The trail to Sunrift Gorge heads north (uphill) along the creek. In about five minutes you will see a small, narrow gorge flanking the creek. Make sure to squeeze up to the very end of the trail to see the waterfall surprise waiting for you at the top end of the gorge.

 Baring, Virginia, and St. Mary Falls

These three waterfall hikes can be combined into one longer hike if you use the shuttle system to drop you off at one end and pick you up on the other. It's tempting to think this will make the hike to all three much more manageable, but it is still a decently long hike for kids (about 2.7 miles each way). If you are up for a hike of this distance, you can save yourself and your kids some energy by hiking it in the downhill direction. Only the most foolish of parents would start at Baring Falls, hike to St. Mary Falls, and then on to Virginia . . . as my notes point out *after* we did it that way! (You benefit from our experience!) The part of the trail between Baring Falls and the cutoff to the St. Mary Shuttle is a climb that took us over an

The trail between Baring and Virginia falls is wide and inviting, but you might also be happy to take advantage of the shuttle.

hour, and the distance shaved off of the St. Mary–Virginia Falls part of the trip is negligible, since the trail from Baring Falls bumps into the other trail only about a quarter of a mile from the road.

Unless you have teens who love to hike, we recommend hiking to Baring Falls and then back to the road, grabbing the shuttle up to the St. Mary Falls parking area, and then hiking to St. Mary and Virginia falls (and all the delightful unnamed falls along the way) together.

You also need to keep in mind that if the weather changes while you are out, as it often does at Glacier, you may be tired and waiting in a downpour of rain. If this unfortunate fate befalls you, do as we did and hop on the first shuttle bus you see, even if it isn't going the direction that you had planned to go! Ride it up to Logan Pass to wait in a slightly less exposed area for the park's next bus going back down.

Baring Falls

This short hike leads through burned forest to a waterfall with an area for snacking or picnicking. Extend the hike by following the trail along the lake to Virginia and St. Mary falls.

Distance: 1 mile round-trip, with 250 feet of elevation gain
Time: 30–60 minutes
Starting point: Take the shuttle or your car to the Sunrift Gorge parking area along Going-to-the-Sun Road. You can park on either side of the road near this area.

The trail to Baring Falls heads south (downhill). If you are on the north side of the road, there is a staircase that takes you down and under the road so you do not have to cross it. If you are on the south side, find another staircase heading down; at the bottom see a sign indicating the trail direction and mileage. Follow the trail downhill, through the 2015 fire burned area; after winding through the woods you'll come out at the falls.

An upside to fires? The profusion of wildflowers that often follows.

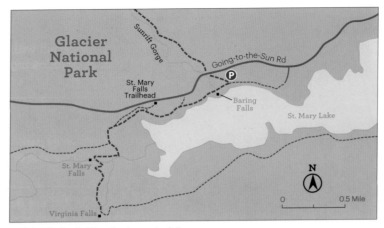

Trail details for St Mary Region waterfalls

 St. Mary Falls

St. Mary Falls is a beautiful double cascade, with a few spots to sit and rest on the rocks nearby. Adding to the attraction of the hike, especially for kids, is the log bridge you cross to reach them.

Distance: From the St. Mary Falls trailhead, it is 0.8 mile to the falls, and then the same heading back, 260 feet of elevation gain in total. See note above about distances from Baring Falls if combining.
Time: 1 hour if going only to St. Mary Falls and back
Starting point: Take the shuttle or your car to the St. Mary Falls trailhead along Going-to-the-Sun Road.

Leave the shuttle stop/parking area and start heading downhill along the trail. After a quarter of a mile, come to the main trail; continue down the trail to the right, following the well-marked signs. (The trail to the left leads to Baring Falls). Your route, however, winds mostly downhill through patches of burned and intact forest to the falls. As you close in on the waterfall, the trail

The gorgeous double cascade of St. Mary Falls

bends to follow the bank of the river. Cross the log bridge across the river to see the falls to your right.

The water is very cold since it is glacial runoff, so we don't really recommend this, but if you have capable and daring children—with personal flotation devices—they can join the ranks of those who jump off the bridge into the obvious deep pool on the downstream side. It's quite exciting to see others do it!

 ## Virginia Falls

Some of the most stunning falls in the park lie along this trail. You will get many more falls than you might expect, if you are willing to put in the time and effort to get out here. An added bonus for the younger set (and the young at heart): rock hopping across a creek. Prepare to get splashed!

Distance: 1.6 miles, out and the same heading back, for a total of 3.2 miles round-trip, with 285 feet of elevation gain. (This includes the St. Mary Falls portion. It is only 0.8 mile beyond St. Mary Falls to Virginia Falls.)

Time: 3–4 hours round-trip

Starting point: Take the shuttle or your car to the Sunrift Gorge parking area along Going-to-the-Sun Road. You can park on either side of the road near this area.

Follow the St. Mary Falls hiking description above for the first section. After leaving St. Mary Falls, the trail starts climbing. At this point you have left behind the burned sections and experience the forest as it was before the fires claimed so much of it. Before long you get a chance to try your hand (or feet) at a creek crossing: rock hopping at its best and a young kid's favorite activity! As you continue along the trail, you are rewarded with multiple unnamed falls.

The first unnamed fall that you come to is off to the left of the trail. The stone formations along the river make natural "steps,"

Even the "secondary" falls en route to Virginia Falls are stunning.

and you will see a distinct "social" trail leading to the falls. Our family could easily have spent all day at these particular falls!

There is a precious little amphitheater carved into the stone just to the right of the falls (probably in early spring the river fills this area as it continues its carving work). It is a wonderful spot to stop and rest. The falls themselves are not spectacular—just a beautiful cascade over orange-colored rocks—but the whole area is just stunning. The kids enjoyed throwing rocks over myriad smaller falls downstream.

Tear yourself away and continue on up the trail to reach the next of the unnamed falls along a much less traveled side trail. We had to climb over some fairly large downed trees to get to the falls themselves. For our kids, climbing over the downed trees is at least as exciting as some old waterfall, if not more! These falls are about 8 feet tall and not easy to get to, but they're beautiful. Once there, you will not find much of a place to sit and relax. Don't worry—more waterfalls ahead!

The next unnamed falls are also a little gem. It is a split falls running over the purple rock of this area. There is more space to sit and relax, but you are also nearing your final destination, and the pull of the big falls is strong!

Continuing onward and upward will lead you to a fork in the trail. This split leads you either to the base of Virginia Falls or to a viewpoint farther up and alongside the falls. If you head left at the split, you will cross a log bridge and come out of the trees with the falls up to your right. There is a huge flat rock area that is perfect for hanging out, and the water below the falls is shallow and slow moving enough to make for fun playing for the kids. You can't really see the entire falls from here, as the top is masked by rock outcroppings.

If you are hoping to find a toilet, a pit toilet also lies in this direction. Unfortunately, when we last used it, it was in terrible shape: small, hot, smelly, dirty, and generally disgusting. Try to avoid using it if at all possible! But if you really must use it, take the trail past the rocky sitting area. It is BYOTP for sure—and you'll also want to hold your breath if you can! Fingers crossed that it's been cleaned up since our visit; if not, let the park service know that it could use some attention.

Back to the fork in the trail . . . if you head to the right, you will come across multiple social trails forking off to the left farther up. These trails lead to various viewpoints, as people are looking for a better and more complete view of the falls; don't take any of them, but instead continue on the main trail until you come to a metal sign with the name of the falls. This last little section, from the bridge below to the viewing area along the top of the falls, is the steepest section. Your little people may be too exhausted to make it this final bit. However, our eleven-year-old bounded right up there and came back reporting that it was "amazing" and said, "You have to go check it out!" And it *was* amazing. You get to feel the spray of the falls as you stand on a huge flat step of a rock. You can see up to the top of the falls and down to the people below, all of which is very exciting for kids, so do what you can to coax your weary troopers to continue.

Enjoy the view and the mist until everyone is recovered from the ascent, then head back down the trail. Depending on the energy of your party—and where you left your car—either return to the split that leads to the St. Mary Falls parking area or pass that by and head all the way to Baring Falls, another mile plus beyond.

We love this hike. It is a long one, and you'll likely need to take a lot of breaks, but there are many wonderful stopping places along the way. Leave plenty of time to enjoy all the falls and to give your kids plenty of rest. Do that, and it is a wonderful trip for everyone in the family.

 Hidden Lake Overlook

Summer comes later to Logan Pass, so you'll likely find plenty of wildflowers here even after they've bloomed out at lower elevations. Add quintessential Glacier Park views, abundant wildlife, and a lake perfect for picnicking, and you've got a dream vacation day.

Distance: 2.8 miles out and back, with an optional 2.4 miles more down to the lake and back, with 460 feet of elevation gain (though it feels like more!)

Time: 1.5–2.5 hours

Starting point: Logan Pass Visitor Center at the top of Going-to-the-Sun Road

Look behind the Logan Pass Visitor Center to find the boardwalk and stair-step trail heading up the alpine tundra. Although you won't find solitude on this hike, there is enough space out here for all. The beginning portion of the hike is on boardwalk that continues to the top of the first ridge.

Along the way you will likely see lots of wildlife, including playful mountain goats. To increase your odds of wildlife sightings, hike in the morning hours. You are most likely to catch an exuberant display of wildflowers if you visit in late summer (late July through August); long after the flowers have faded away at lower elevations, the cooler climes on Logan Pass are

Hidden Lake from the overlook boardwalk

warming just enough to encourage the vast array of flowering plants to burst into full bloom.

After cresting the ridge, the boardwalk path ends, as does most of the elevation gain. The gentle rolling trail, made of packed earth scattered with rock and gravel, is easy to spot and follow. The scene greeting you at the end of the boardwalk beckons you on to catch glimpses of more wildlife and small alpine lakes and peaks soaring impossibly higher. Keep an eye out for more mountain goats tucked into the small copses of alpine trees or crossing the trail ahead of you.

In a short while you reach Hidden Lake Overlook, where you can look down on the lake's shockingly blue waters nestled amid a grand wilderness of rock. There is a bit more boardwalk and some rock uprisings you can sit on but not a lot of space for picnicking. The smaller forest critters seem to know this is a popular stopping and snacking place and are bold and obnoxious if you try to eat here. Remember, for their safety and yours, they should not be fed or touched!

After taking in the scenery and snapping some photos, you can choose to descend the 780 vertical feet of trail to the lake itself or turn around and head back. If you are trying to see more than the Logan Pass area in one day, we recommend hiking back now, but if you have more time and want to head down to the lake, get an early start so you have plenty of time to get to the lake (and back again) and enjoy your time on the shores of Hidden Lake. While wonderfully refreshing to dip feet in, this lake is probably too cold for actual swimming.

 Highline Trail to Haystack Pass

Big views, abundant wildflowers, and a cliff-face traverse make this a most memorable trail. Keep in mind that the western exposure of this trail means that you get a lot of sun in the afternoon. An early morning start brings shaded hiking and fewer people; an afternoon hike yields warmer temperatures and more sun, as well as more people on this popular trail.

Distance: 7.2 miles round-trip, with 825 feet of elevation gain
Time: 3–6 hours
Starting point: Logan Pass parking area

The features that make this hike memorable also make it popular; you will want to start early or consider using the shuttle to access this trail because the parking lot is often full. The trailhead is just across Going-to-the-Sun Road from the Logan Pass Visitor Center. Start on the trail as it winds down through a series of small meadows where you have a good chance of spotting bighorn sheep and mountain goats.

Just beyond the meadows, you reach the big test of your nerves—a famous section of trail that is etched out of the cliff face. Here, the trail is about 4–6 feet wide, and the downhill side plummets almost vertically down 100 feet to Going-to-the-Sun Road. It is bound to get your attention, but the trail is flat and stable with a cable to hold onto if you feel nervous, so actual danger is low if you simply pay attention to what you're doing. And we believe you will! For the most part, kids love the thrill of this part of the hike. Honestly assess your children's abilities though, and keep close to them along this section.

The section is just 0.3 mile long, so scoot across and quickly put your fear of heights behind you as you continue on to other memorable sections of the trail. For the next 2 miles, the trail undulates gently along what is known as the Garden Wall because of the abundant wildflowers and greenery of this gorgeous alpine environment. The rock spires above you comprise the spine of the Continental Divide, and numerous small streams trickle down, providing the water needed by the flowers, while the slope's westerly aspect provides abundant sunlight. The result is that your party seldom travels more than a few hundred yards without encountering some new wildflower to view, marvel at, and photograph. The variety, frequency, and proximity of the flowers is ideal for kids' short attention spans.

We highly recommend hiking at least this far. You won't regret the experience and you will have walked the best-known

The Highline Trail can test your nerves, but it is worth it.

sections of the trail, so go just as far as your family feels comfortable and then turn around and head back.

But if you continue farther, look left and be rewarded with an unending supply of beautiful views of Mount Cannon, Mount Oberlin, and Heavens Peak. Eventually you enter a large alpine bowl that is a bit gentler in slope. The trail first contours around this huge meadow; on the far side it starts the only serious climb of the trip in one large switchback.

At the top of this switchback lies Haystack Pass, roughly half the distance to Granite Park Chalet and another good turnaround point. The views off either side are breathtaking, and a few relatively flat areas and large boulders provide a good picnic site. Spend as much time here as your muscles desire and the weather permits, and then retrace your steps back to Logan Pass to enjoy the amazing views all over again. Keep in mind that kids might be weary on the return trip, so keep an extra watchful eye on them along the steep portion of the trail.

Mount Oberlin Climbers Route

A side trail that climbers use to reach the surrounding peaks and hikers use to reach some prime mountain goat habitat, the full length of this strenuous route is not for everyone. The first section, however, is easily accessible, with expansive views, water features, and good opportunities to view wildlife.

Distance: Less than 1 mile round-trip, with minimal elevation gain
Time: 30–90 minutes
Starting point: Logan Pass Visitor Center

If the boardwalk trail to Hidden Lake overlook is crammed with people and you'd like to avoid the crowds, or if you would like more opportunities to view mountain goats and possibly bighorn sheep, then this short jaunt could be just the ticket. The park service does everything it can to avoid cross-country travel in this fragile ecosystem, but also wants to provide rock climbers with access to some of the impressive peaks in this area. As a result, two trails in the Logan Pass area provide access to the peaks, established over routes chosen to avoid sensitive alpine vegetation, sticking to less fragile, rockier areas.

The closer and easier of the two is the Oberlin Route, which is little known to the nonclimbers and travels through excellent sheep and goat habitat. The trail begins off an oval-shaped, paved interpretive walk just north of the Logan Pass Visitor Center. As you walk around the interpretive trail, you will see a well-defined trail leaving it in approximately the 10 o'clock position. A chain barrier stretched around the perimeter of the paved trail in this area is intended to discourage overland travel, but we've confirmed that stepping over the chain to access this trail is permitted.

The trail begins amid a narrow and beautiful wildflower meadow (stay on the path!) and then turns left and starts climbing. Soon you come to a water tank and intake pipes which

Looking back toward Logan Pass on the Mount Oberlin Climbers Route

provide the water that supports the visitor center. The trail becomes fainter and veers to the right toward a red rock cliff face with a cascading waterfall. We saw numerous mountain goats in this area and hope you will too, but even without the animals this is a fun stream for kids to play in and be "brave" while crossing using the larger flat rocks as stepping stones.

The trail actually crosses the stream below the waterfall and then climbs a bit up and to the left as it enters a small forest of stunted, windblown trees (the term for this is "krummholz forest"). At this point it levels out again as it winds through alternating meadows and krummholz for a couple of hundred yards.

This is a good spot to turn around if you have seen enough goats and taken enough photos; from here the route begins to climb to the ridge between Oberlin and Clements mountains and becomes rockier and steeper. Head back the way you came, happy to have avoided the crowds this time.

Granite Park from the Loop Trailhead

Older, capable children who are looking for a little more challenge in their outing will appreciate this route to a beautiful alpine bowl, historic chalet, and incredible views. Hiking to the Granite Park Chalet and spending the night there instead of in a tent is a great option—but you'll have to plan ahead for it. The trail lacks shade much of the time so get an early start if you can.

Distance: 4.2 miles each way, 2450 feet of elevation gain
Time: 4–8 hours
Starting point: The Loop Trailhead on Going-to-the-Sun Road, 13.1 miles east of the Lake McDonald Lodge. The Loop Trailhead is a shuttle stop located on a distinctive 180-degree bend in the road.

The trail leaves the road and crosses a bridge almost immediately after you leave the trailhead, and then spends the first 0.6 mile gently undulating along the contour of the mountain until it intersects the Packers Roost Trail; keep right at the junction. Consider this first part of the trail as a warm-up (or for the little kids, a test ground) for what lies ahead. Shortly after the junction, the trail starts to get serious about gaining elevation. For the first two-thirds of this trip you are walking through remains of the large, lightning-caused Trapper Creek forest fire of 2003. Enough time has passed that there is abundant green undergrowth, wildflowers, and young trees rising up from the devastation, but thousands of ghostly white trunks are a testimony to what happened here years ago. The bad news is that the young trees are not yet tall enough to provide shade. The good news is that mature trees no longer block views of the impressive 8987-foot Heavens Peak to the west—and the dead snags provide habitat for woodpeckers and other wildlife. The higher you go, the broader the vistas become.

After 2.8 miles the trail enters a lush, more mature forest, with glimpses above to the peaks and basins of the Garden Wall along the Continental Divide. As you move deeper into the

The views only improve as you get higher on the Granite Park Trail.

forest, the trail starts to level out in places, and small verdant meadows appear in the clearings. Keep looking up and you will soon spot the chalet above that marks your destination; as you get closer to the top, expansive views of the lower end of the park open up. For kids, seeing the chalet in the distance gives them a reference point for the never-ending question, "Are we there yet?"

At the next trail junction, going right leads to the Grinnell Glacier Overlook and the Highline trail back to Logan Pass; straight heads to Swiftcurrent Pass and, eventually, the Many Glacier area. Turn left for at least a quick visit to Granite Park Chalet. This classic chalet was built in 1915 by the Great Northern Railroad to provide comfortable accommodations in the park.

The chalet offers the services that you'd expect from a rustic hikers hostel. Inside are bunk beds but no electric light or running water (although there is a natural spring water source about a 5-minute walk from the chalet). It does have a propane stove in the common area kitchen, so if you have planned to stay overnight, you are spared the necessity of carrying a tent and cooking equipment; you have a sheltered space to prepare your meals and sleep at night. For more details on using the chalet, see the Glacier Camping and Lodging chapter.

But maybe a night at the chalet isn't in the cards, or you and the kids still have some energy to burn. At this point the climbing is behind you, but you could put in a little more trail time. The hike to the Grinnell Glacier overlook is only 1.5 miles from the chalet, and half of that is level. The trail is visible from the chalet. Head back to the junction to take the short trip to Swiftcurrent Pass.

On one of our visits, we planned to hike to the overlook and started down that trail at a fast pace. We soon encountered a breathless hiker, coming from the other direction, who asked if we had bear spray! Looking ahead about 200 yards we saw a beautiful mother grizzly and her yearling cub. These bears had been frequenting the area that summer, and the mother was nicknamed "Blondie." From this distance, they posed no immediate threat, but they were in no hurry to go anywhere either. They soon climbed up on the trail and started ambling down the trail, roughly toward us, at an easy pace, stopping to feed on low-lying berries and digging for ground squirrels. The strength of the mother bear as she tore with her massive claws at the earth was impressive, and created no desire to get any closer. It soon became apparent that the delays caused by her presence no longer left time to reach the overlook. We turned around, disappointed at not being able to see Grinnell Glacier from above but excited to have seen a mama grizzly bear up close—but not too close!

Adventures Beyond Hiking

Adding more adventure to your trip means more engagement and interest from your kids, and there are some decent options in this region of the park. While cycling (aside from riding around in the campground) and horseback riding aren't feasible here, there are some great opportunities to get on the water and, depending on your energy levels, to do some sightseeing by bus.

Boating

While you can bring your own craft (see Boating in the Planning Your Glacier Family Vacation chapter for requirements and restrictions), the St. Mary and Logan Pass Region also offers some excellent options. If you want a relaxing water tour, get tickets to ride aboard one of the tour boats operated by the Glacier Park Boat Company (see Resources). The *Little Chief* leaves out of the Rising Sun boat dock, about 5 miles up the Going-to-the-Sun Road from the St. Mary entrance station. Tours on St. Mary Lake can be 1.5 hours long or 3.5 with a guided hike along the way. There is another dock along the shore where the trail between Baring Falls and Virginia Falls meets the shoreline. This dock is a drop-off and pick-up point for hikers.

The *Little Chief* approaches the boat dock.

The lake portion of the tour takes you by the famous Goose Island, many other tiny islands in the lake, the Sexton Glacier, and 360-degree views of the surrounding mountains. Similar to the boat tour on Lake McDonald, we don't really recommend this tour for most kids—unless you plan to take the hike partway through. We find that kids aren't particularly enthused about sitting on a boat for an hour and a half looking at scenery, even if the scenery is interesting. We think your kids will have more fun exploring on foot in this particular region of the park, but if the adults in your group really want to experience St. Mary Lake by boat, consider giving the kids cameras to document the ride. Having a camera will engage them in their surroundings more deeply, which makes the ride more fun! Prices and timetables are available at Glacier Park Boat Company (see Resources). Reservations require advance purchase, though a portion of the tickets are reserved as walk-ups. These can be claimed up to three days in advance.

Bus Touring
You will find all three bus/tour options originating from the St. Mary area. The park's free shuttle bus can take you from the St. Mary Visitor Center up to Logan Pass with stops at all the popular hiking spots along the way. The Sun Tour buses depart from St. Mary each morning. The Red Bus tours also depart from the St. Mary area, offering four different tour options. See Bus Touring in the Planning Your Glacier Family Vacation chapter for more info on each type of tour and the Resources section for how to contact them and make reservations.

Services and Amenities
As the hub for activities on the east side of the park, St. Mary is where you will find most services and amenities. Just outside the entrance station is the small town of St. Mary, with groceries, lodging, gas, and information. Immediately inside the entrance station is the St. Mary Visitor Center, with bathrooms, books, interpretive information, maps, souvenirs,

national parks passport stamps, and park rangers willing to answer questions.

MANY GLACIER REGION

When someone mentions Glacier National Park, what image comes to mind? Likely the image you conjure up will be something that you would find in Many Glacier. This region is the epitome of what we are protecting in Glacier National Park. There are glaciers, of course, but also glacial lakes, wildlife,

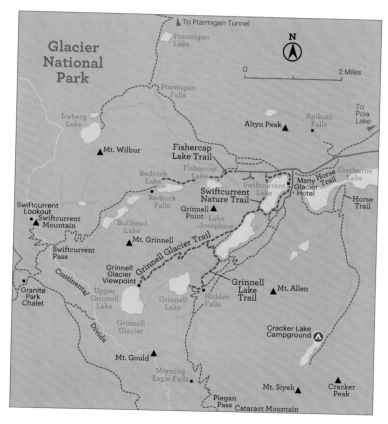

impressive falls, and massive mountains. Near the roads, the region is quite developed, and unlike some of the other, more remote regions, there are still plenty of services available to make your stay as comfortable as you would like. Yet the trails can take you to undeveloped, wild places. In Many Glacier, you really have it all!

Things You Need to Know

The views here are quintessential Glacier Park; some are offered from the old-time comfort of the stunning Many Glacier Hotel. Many Glacier is also prime territory for moose and offers a great chance of seeing them. In this region you will find adventures for all abilities and views all ages can appreciate.

Hiking Adventures

Hiking in the Many Glacier area will take you from civilization to wilderness faster than any other area of the park. This makes it a great place for families! You can stay in an area with ample resources for a comfortable stay but still get your kids out into the woods to explore and experience wildlife.

 Apikuni Falls

Delayed gratification is the order of the day on this arduous hike. Stick it out and you'll be rewarded with big views of the Many Glacier Valley, beautiful falls, a tumbling creek, and a glowing sense of accomplishment.

Distance: 2 miles out and back, with an elevation gain of 700 feet
Time: 1.5–2.5 hours
Starting point: Trailhead parking area about 1 mile east of the Many Glacier Hotel on the Many Glacier entrance road, north side of the road

---

The trail to Apikuni Falls begins with a moderate uphill, but the incline quickly increases. Prepare yourself and the kids for a strenuous climb that might feel longer than it is, most of the

You can see both the lower and upper Apikuni falls simultaneously.

way to the falls. The trail enters a forest of mixed aspen and coniferous trees shortly after leaving the trailhead and stays in the trees for most of the hike, with views appearing only near the top.

After you've traveled about three-quarters of a mile, winding your way through the forest, side trails start spurring off the main trail. These social trails lead to the creek as it tumbles down the mountain you are climbing. Resist that temptation and keep to the main trail, but make sure to take breaks as needed to refresh and refuel tired kids along the way.

Eventually, breaks in the forest allow views out behind you and a glimpse of the falls in the distance towering above you. Keep climbing. Soon you emerge at the boulder-strewn creek and many small falls. Apikuni Falls is still above you, but it's much closer than before. This is a great spot to stop and snack, rest, let the kids play, and admire the upper falls. For a closer view, there is a rocky, gravelly goat path of a trail that leads to the base of the main falls. If you opt to take it, be careful, and remember that it's always easier to go up a treacherous route than to come back down it.

When you've had your fill, head back down the trail, happy in the knowledge that it will take you quite a bit less time and effort to return than it took you to ascend.

 Redrock Lake and Falls

Travel along the shores of two lakes to the stunning Redrock Falls, with close-in views of the surrounding high mountains. Young kids will want to linger by the lake, while older kids will enjoy exploring around the falls. Everyone will appreciate the mostly level trail.

Distance: 3.6 miles round-trip, with 200 feet of elevation gain
Time: 2.5–3.5 hours

Don't let a little damp weather dampen your spirits on the trail to Redrock Lake and Falls.

Starting point: Trailhead is located at the back of the parking lot for the Swiftcurrent Motor Inn and store, adjacent to the Many Glacier Campground.

Beginning in the woods, and remaining among the trees for much of the time, the trail winds through young forest as it rises and falls past Fishercap Lake (for optional spur trail to this lake, see description below) and then overland to the shores of

Redrock Lake. The gently rolling terrain and the mixed shade and sun make this a pleasant trail that kids will enjoy.

Beyond Fishercap Lake the way begins to climb moderately and the forest opens up a bit, with views of some huge peaks, including Mount Wilbur and Mount Henkel, rising around you, as well as views of the shore of Redrock Lake and the falls. A small beach at the lake makes a nice stopping place. Let your kids skip stones on the lake and recharge with a snack.

Continue on around Redrock Lake toward the falls. It's not far; another 15 minutes of hiking will get you to your destination.

The falls themselves are largely obscured by the huge, red boulders littering the trail. Scramble around as much as you are comfortable, until you can get a good view and find a place to relax a bit. You can make your way toward the bottom of the falls or climb your way up around the top. There are some great opportunities for older kids to explore here, but keep in mind that the water is very cold and you are some distance from emergency care.

After enjoying these snapshot-worthy falls, make your way back to the trailhead the way you came.

 Fishercap Lake

Shhhhh! This short jaunt to a shallow lake provides excellent opportunities to view moose feeding on the aquatic plants ... if you're both lucky and quiet.

Distance: 1.5 miles out and back, with minimal elevation gain
Time: 30–60 minutes
Starting point: Trailhead is located at the back of the parking lot for the Swiftcurrent Motor Inn and store, adjacent to the Many Glacier Campground.

This hike is pretty short and relatively flat. About 0.2 mile from the trailhead, look for a turn to the lake on your left. You will drop down and later have to hike back up, but the elevation

Grinnell is reflected in Fishercap Lake on a sunny day. (iStock/Richard Seeley photo)

change is minimal and the footing good. Keep very quiet as you hike down toward the lake, as this site is an excellent spot to see wildlife, particularly moose.

All of Fishercap Lake is extremely shallow, but with lots of sun, the aquatic plants flourish, which makes the moose happy. Those plants are favored browse for moose, and they can often be seen here munching on this delicious (to moose) food. In the spring, you may see a moose calf if you are patient: often the cow moose will hide her calf on the shore until she is sure it is safe to emerge. A ranger described how mother moose lead their calves out into the shallow water to browse and protect them from grizzly bears. Bring a snack and be prepared to sit for a bit as you wait to enjoy some great wildlife viewing!

Grinnell Lake

Make use of the boat shuttle to make this most enjoyable hike; it has little elevation gain and wends through a mature forest to glacial Grinnell Lake, far below Grinnell Glacier, and surrounded by impressive peaks.

Distance: 2.2 miles round-trip from concession's boat dock; 6.8 miles out and back from Grinnell Glacier trailhead, with minimal elevation gain
Time: 2–3 hours from boat dock trailhead; 4–6 hours from trailhead near lodge
Starting point: It's possible to hike this trail from the Grinnell Glacier trailhead near the Many Glacier Hotel, but we recommend that families use the concession's boat service, saving 5 miles of lakeside hiking.

After an informative boat ride on two vessels across two lakes (see the Boating section), hike along a mostly level 1.1-mile trail that cuts through thick brush, traversing seasonal streams. The trail is often boardwalk, and you'll frequently share it with other

The mirror-like waters of Grinnell Lake lend themselves to reflection.

hikers. It is a good idea to make some noise as you walk—not usually a challenge when hiking with kids!—as there are also often bears in the area and it's easy to surprise them (and they surprise you) in the thick brush. This is also excellent moose habitat. (The same safety rules follow for moose: if you come across one on a trail, make sure to slowly back away, not proceeding until the moose leaves.) Our children found the trail easy and enjoyed the mix of trail and boardwalk.

The trail sort of dumps you out onto the lakeshore, where you can spread out for a snack or picnic and some rest. Kids can usually find endless fun along the shores of a lake, so plan to spend a bit of time here. Grinnell Glacier is visible, hanging in a glacial valley far above the lake, and you can also see an impressive waterfall on the cliffs between the glacier, Upper Grinnell Lake, and Grinnell Lake.

Two notes: First, the boat tour offers guided hikes to Grinnell Lake on some of its trips. You can plan ahead to join one, if you like to have a tour guide. We find that the tour guide pace isn't usually the pace kids want to walk, so we sometimes just pop in and out of the tour group as we go. Second, if some members of your party are more physically fit and would like to hike to the glacier, you can split up after the boat ride at the top of Lake Josephine—there are two trails, one to Grinnell Lake and the other to Upper Grinnell Lake and Grinnell Glacier (see next hike). That is what our family did. It was nice to take the boat rides together but also satisfying for each group to have the hiking experience that worked for them.

 Grinnell Glacier

A big hike with big rewards—there are amazing views every step of the way, frequent wildlife sightings, beautiful lakes, and an up-close view of a glacier to cap it all off. If you do just one big hike in Glacier, this is the one to do. Just be sure to check trail status, as this trail can still have snow into July.

Distance: 7.6 miles round-trip, with 1840 feet of elevation gain from the boat dock

Time: 4.5–7 hours

Starting point: Find the trailhead at the boat dock at the south end of Lake Josephine.

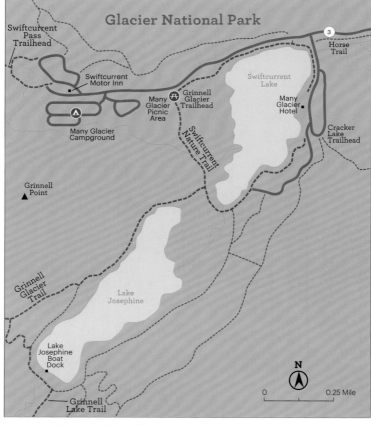

Road and trail detail for Many Glacier Region

The Grinnell Glacier Trail offers some fine views.

The distance and elevation gain on this hike make it the most challenging you'll find in this book, but by most accounts this is also the top-rated hike in the park. The statistics listed above assume that you begin and end your hike by taking the shuttle boat across the two lakes. Skipping the shuttle adds another 3.6 miles to your journey, through less interesting terrain.

Leaving the trailhead at the end of the lake, the trail hooks around to cross Grinnell Lake's outlet stream before beginning to climb 0.4 mile to join the Josephine Lake Trail. At the trail junction, turn left (west) and begin hiking up the canyon toward the glacier and the Continental Divide.

The trail in this section is moderate and in good condition and climbs at a steady rate. Soon you will have delightful views to your left as you leave the valley floor, including down toward Grinnell Lake and across to the wonderful series of cascading waterfalls on the slopes above it. The lake is glacier fed, giving it that now familiar turquoise color that never ceases to amaze visitors of all stripes.

As you come alongside the lake (though still far above it) you won't exactly leave the forest entirely, but the trees will become shorter and gnarled and the terrain more open. Terraced bands of red rock emerge, interspersed with grassy benches; this is a good area to see bighorn sheep.

Continue to climb. The trail narrows as it reaches a band of cliff faces, with small waterfalls trickling down the walls that frame the trail. At one point, you are climbing up rock steps as the water splashes down on you from the side, making for a memorable hike! The trail here has steep drop-offs in places and wet, potentially slippery rocks due to all the water. Keep it from becoming *too* memorable by keeping your eyes on the trail instead of constantly craning at the amazing views across the valley. That said, do take the time to look back down the valley at the lakes from whence you came; the panorama is gorgeous.

This section continues for quite a while, and you can mark your progress as you near the top of the waterfalls that you've been watching. The trail steepens further as it enters the glacial cirque that holds Grinnell Glacier, but persevere; your goal is now getting quite close. With the massive cliff walls approaching and encircling you, as you finally crest the last hill you will suddenly see a blue lake with a lot of floating icebergs within it and the namesake Grinnell Glacier looming above. Congratulations, you've made it!

We suggest eating your pack lunch on the rock shelves overlooking the lake. The views are fabulous; don't forget to look back over the terrain that you climbed to get here. The route back is the same trail that you traveled up on.

Consider an early start to Grinnell Glacier, because the beauty of this trail also makes it popular, and you'll encounter fewer crowds if you hike up in the morning hours. In fact, waiting for people going the opposite direction on some of the narrower sections of trail is one of the variables in how long this hike will take. Also, bringing extra insulation layers is a key to comfort, because it is sure to be cooler up top. Conversely, on warm, sunny days the trail offers little in the way of shade; it is exposed to the sun for the entire route, so sunscreen is a must.

Leaving early also increases your chances of seeing wildlife, whether it is moose in the valley below, sheep and goats on the steep rocks above, or bears in the alpine area above tree line—or really anywhere. Give yourselves plenty of time, because it is a long trail and you'll want to stop often to soak in the views and take pictures. Thanks to the variety and beauty of this area, it's not a bad idea to plan to spend a full day on this hike.

 ## Swiftcurrent Nature Trail

Looking for an easy stroll that you can tailor to fit the amount of time you have? How about adding in some possible moose sightings? Swiftwater Lake is the destination for you!

Distance: 2.4 miles around the lake, or turn around whenever you want, with no elevation gain

Time: 1.5 hours or less

Starting point: Leave from the Grinnell Glacier trailhead and parking area off the Many Glacier Entrance Road.

Who doesn't love a nature trail that starts out level and easy to follow, and stays that way for the entire loop? Kids will enjoy

Sometimes you want a pretty hike with no elevation gain: Swiftcurrent Nature Trail delivers.

the easy nature of the path, as well as the opportunity to throw stones in the lake periodically. And they might see moose. Leaving from the Grinnell Glacier trailhead, the path heads toward the lake and away from the hotel. The first quarter of a mile is wheelchair accessible as it winds through the woods to a bridge and river crossing, which can be entertaining for kids. The trail continues, mostly through forest but with sightings of the lake, for another 0.8 mile. At this point you will see a side trail to the right, leading to Lake Josephine and the boat dock, just over the rise, but continue on the main trail for 0.2 mile to reach a larger creek entering from the right through a swampy area. This spot offers great potential to see moose, especially early or late in the day.

From here it is another 0.7 mile to continue around the lake to the hotel, or 1.5 miles to your car and the trailhead. Or you can turn around and walk the mile back the way you came.

Adventures Beyond Hiking

Hiking is obviously just about our favorite thing to do in Glacier National Park, but there are many other excellent ways to experience the Many Glacier Region.

Horseback Rides

Atop the back of a horse is a wonderful way to see the great outdoors. In Glacier National Park the concessioner for this type of adventure is Swan Mountain Outfitters. They offer a variety of rides in the Many Glacier area and welcome children age eight and up for one- and two-hour rides, half-day rides, and all-day packages that include both riding horses and a boat tour with some free time in between. Check out their website for prices and further details and to make reservations (see Resources).

Bicycling

There are no formal bike trails in the Many Glacier area, but your family may find it convenient to ride bikes along the main road system from one trailhead to another, eliminating the

The *Morning Eagle* plies the waters of Lake Josephine.

frustrating problem of trying to find a parking space. If you do, keep in mind that road shoulders are abrupt, and many drivers have their eyes on the the scenery or looking for wildlife, not paying attention to the road or families on bikes. Follow all traffic laws, stay alert, and always wear a helmet!

Boating

Getting on the water is a great way to enjoy the Many Glacier Region. If you're interested in bringing your own craft, read the Boating section in the Planning Your Glacier Family Vacation chapter, but our recommendation is to take advantage of the rides that are commercially available on Swiftcurrent Lake and Lake Josephine. Travel on one of the tour boats operated by the Glacier Park Boat Company (see Resources), and access trailheads at the same time. You can even ride the *Chief Two Guns* across Swiftcurrent Lake (starting at the dock outside the Many Glacier Hotel), disembark on the far shore, then hike a short smooth path over the hill and climb aboard the *Morning Eagle* to continue your boat tour on Lake Josephine! The second boat takes you to the top of the lake, where you can head off on hikes to Grinnell Lake and Grinnell Glacier, saving you miles of hiking—and giving you some boating with a purpose beyond sightseeing.

Bus Touring

Unlike other areas of the park, the Many Glacier Region offers no free shuttle bus. If you are interested in a tour, you can choose from three different Red Bus Tours. There are Sun Tours on this side of the park, but none originate here. To join one, you will need to meet up with them in St. Mary. Find more details on bus touring in the Planning Your Glacier Family Vacation chapter and check out Resources for contact information for reservations.

Services and Amenities

The Many Glacier Region boasts plenty of amenities to cover the needs of most families. There are many lodging options (see the Glacier Camping and Lodging chapter) and several restaurants, including in the Many Glacier Hotel and the Swiftcurrent Motor Inn, which has a camp store and gift shop on site as well. The Swiftcurrent Motor Inn offers access to a shower even if you're not staying there, a luxury not always available to campers in our national parks. Finally, each of the concessioners has representatives here—for horseback riding, boating, and motor coach tours. There are no visitor centers in the region; if you are looking for books, maps, or permits, you will need to stop in at one of the other visitor centers, the closest being in St. Mary, 21 miles away to the south.

TWO MEDICINE REGION

Due to its kid friendliness and relief from the crowds, Two Medicine is our favorite region of Glacier. Before Going-to-the-Sun Road was opened to motorized traffic, Two Medicine was one of the more popular regions in the park. It features hiking to beautiful places with lots of features for kids to enjoy, a roomy campground, and amenities like boat tours and a camp store, with far fewer people. Additionally, the campground is situated just before Two Medicine Lake and a little creek that runs into

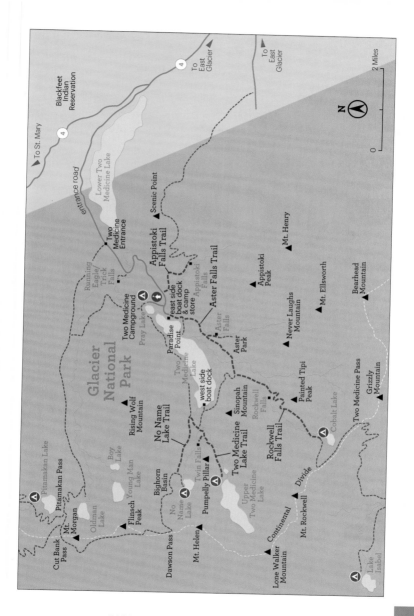

an adjacent, smaller lake, Pray Lake. The small lake's water is cold but shallow, and kids can spend hours playing on the shores or wading on a hot day. The hiking here is fantastic and mellow, with waterfalls aplenty, high mountain lakes without the big elevation gains, and a quiet sense of peacefulness. This is also the region in which we found the best backpacking options for families; see details in the chapter Your First Glacier Backpacking Trip. We think you will love bringing your family to "Two Med."

Things You Need to Know

As mentioned above, this region is a bit more remote than the other, more developed regions of the park. While good for escaping the crowds, this does mean less access to services. Sometimes that can be difficult when camping with children, but fortunately, there is a camp store with the basics. Plan on coming prepared to rough it, and you can have a great time with your kids here.

Another great advantage for adventuring in Two Med is the use of the boat tour up Two Medicine Lake to shave miles off your hikes and gain access to beautiful and enjoyable adventures beyond the lake. The boating here is the best value in the park, so make sure to take advantage of it if you are visiting here.

In the hike descriptions that follow, we point you to the appropriate boat dock for those hikes that start with a boat ride. A trailhead starting point is given for hikes that start on a trail. The "South Shore Trailhead" is located near Two Medicine Lake's east-side boat dock.

Hiking Adventures

 Appistoki Falls

It isn't our favorite hike in the Two Medicine region of the park, but who wouldn't be excited about sharing the trail with bighorn sheep? If you need a short hike that's still a

The saddle along the hike to Appistoki Falls offers a peek into the backcountry—and possibly a view of bighorn sheep.

bit of a challenge to start or finish your day, take the trail to Appistoki Falls.

Distance: 1.2 miles round-trip, with 260 feet of elevation gain
Time: 45–90 minutes
Starting point: A quarter of a mile before you arrive at the ranger station on the Two Medicine Entrance Road, as you come in to the park; park in the "Scenic Point" parking area.

The trail begins as a rolling path in the subalpine forest, but quickly gains elevation as you follow Appistoki Creek. As you begin to climb, you encounter a split in the trail. Both trails meet up again near the falls, but we recommend the right branch, as it stays closer to the water and you will have an easier time spotting the falls as you close in on them.

After climbing for about 0.4 mile, the trail is high above the level of the creek below, and you soon catch a glimpse of the falls ahead of you and off to the side, deep in the ravine. There is no really good viewpoint at which to stop and rest to observe the falls—the one great limitation of this hike. Continue to just past where the trail branches join together again to reach a level bench with sweeping views all around.

This area is also a good place to look for bighorn sheep, which seem to use the trail as much as people do. We were lucky enough to see a group of about fifteen sheep coming through the trees as we sat quietly, watching them from just 15 yards away as they headed down the trail. The experience was a thrill for all of us, young and old.

You can keep going if you like (it's another 3.3 miles and about 2300 feet of elevation to a scenic high point), or turn around here and head back. We took the other side of the earlier split in the trail on the way down to change up the scenery, but either way will get you back. While overall this hike didn't rank high on our "fun for kids" list—the trail is steep and water out of reach—it's a good option if you are looking for a chance to see some wildlife if your kids don't mind a bit of elevation gain.

 ### Running Eagle (Trick) Falls

This short hike is popular for good reason. It is worth braving the crowds to visit these stunning falls—especially in the spring when the runoff from snowmelt makes them spectacular. At that time of year, one fall of water shoots off the top of the rocky outcrop while another seemingly emerges out of the rocks below. You really must see it to believe it!

Distance: 0.6 mile round trip, with no elevation gain, handicap accessible
Time: 15–30 minutes
Starting point: Running Eagle Falls trailhead (east of the camping area) off the Two Medicine Entrance Road

---

Shortly after beginning down the trail, you will see another trail branching off to the left. It is labeled as the "nature trail," but you want to stay on the main trail to go to the falls. Before long, this forest of brush and scrub trees is left behind and you

One of the "trick" aspects of the falls: the water appears to flow out of the rock wall.

emerge onto the gravelly banks of a river. You can "rock hop" the river most times of the year (fun for the kids too!), but if the river is running high, in late spring or on bright days triggering snowmelt, you may need to head upstream along the bank to reach the bridge.

There are many delightful spots to sit and relax and view these tricksy falls. Bring a snack or lunch and plan to spend time here, especially if you have small kids who like to play at the water's edge. The rocky creek bed and clear waters of this area make for delightful streamside play. We give this hike a high rating as a kid-friendly, adult-interest hike.

Aster Falls and Aster Park Overlook

A winding trail through the woods leads to delightful falls and, for those willing to expend the effort, big views of the Two Medicine area. Whether you go the full distance to the view or are contented to stay at the falls, you'll want your camera for sure.

A snack break at the foot of Aster Falls

Distance: 2.8 miles round-trip to the falls, with 320 feet of elevation gain; 4 miles round-trip to the park, with an additional 460 feet of elevation gain

Time: 3–4 hours to the falls, 4–5 hours to the park

Starting point: East-side boat dock on Two Medicine Lake

The trail rolls its way slowly from the shores of the lake, entering forest, but before you leave the shores behind entirely you will see the turnoff to Paradise Point. Make a note of that for a future hike (see below), but continue on the main trail now. After about 30 minutes you come to some beaver ponds among the trees and then some larger ponds in a meadow area. This is a wonderful place to see moose, especially if you are here early in the morning or just before dusk. If you just want to look for animals, hiking only this far would be a great option. On one of our visits, we were also fortunate enough to see a male blue grouse showing off for a group of females in this area.

After this wildlife meadow, reenter the trees and hike until you see the signed split in the trail. Here you can go left and down to Aster Falls or continue right to head straight to the Aster Park overlook. Take the left fork to the delightful falls. Initially you get only a glimpse of the lower portion of the falls, but keep going. Look for some very large, flat rocks in the center of the water channel, and hop out onto them for an excellent view of the entire falls.

Water cascades down tier upon tier of rocks in a series of little falls. The large rocks at the base, dappled by shade and sunlight, make a wonderful stopping spot. Pull out drinks and a snack, and sit and enjoy the falls. Your kids will find much to keep them busy exploring in the wide, slow area of the river by which you are sitting. There are wildflowers all around the edges of the river. It is a truly enchanting spot, well worth the effort for both kids and adults alike.

The one drawback is that due to the relative shortness of the trail and the beauty of the destination, Aster Falls is bound to be a busy spot on many a summer day. On an overcast day with sprinkling rain, you might find relatively very few people, but on a sunny day this spot sees more traffic.

At this point you may want to divide your party, sending the hardier hikers on to the overlook while the younger ones hang with mom or dad to stay at the creek. The trail to Aster Park continues on, leaving the valley floor to gain about 460 feet in less than a mile through a series of switchbacks. Though relatively short, it's a bit of a leg burner, but as you break out of the trees at the top, you are rewarded with commanding views of the surrounding stellar area.

 Paradise Point

A short hike to a more remote part of Two Medicine Lake's shoreline, with views farther up the lake, Paradise Point is a perfect destination if you have small, non-hiking kids but want to get away from the "civilization" of the boathouse and parking areas.

Distance: 0.5 mile, with no elevation gain
Time: 30 minutes
Starting point: East-side boat dock on Two Medicine Lake

Begin along the trail to Aster Falls and Park, but before long (at 0.2 mile), you'll see a trail to the right that heads back down toward the lakeshore. Take that path, and after a semi-steep descent with fortunately good tread, come out of the trees into a marshy area. Here the trail rises onto boardwalks that keep your footing dry and secure. After traversing several of these boardwalks, you reach the lakeshore once more. This is Paradise Point, and it provides some winning views farther up Two Medicine Lake that you cannot see from the parking area or boathouse. At a rocky shore composed of smooth river rocks, take a snack break and allow plenty of time for rock skipping. Once you've had your fill, head back the way you came.

The view up Two Medicine Lake from Paradise Point

 Rockwell Falls

Majestic multitiered falls perfect for exploring, rock scrambling, and relaxing with older children: this hike is a must-do for families with kids who are good hikers and climbers. If your kids aren't to that age yet, consider whether one of the parents or guardians could sneak away for a morning or an afternoon. Even though the focus of this book is what kids will like, we adults love some adventure too, including the thrill of discovery and the chance to take in beauty in semi-remote backcountry. Whether you go with or without your kids, Rockwell Falls is well worth your effort!

Distance: 4.4 miles out and back from boat dock at the western end of the lake, 7 miles out and back from the South Shore trailhead, with 375 feet of elevation gain
Time: 2.5–4.5 hours
Starting point: South Shore trailhead for hiking or west-end boat dock on Two Medicine Lake, if riding the *Sinopah*

The trail leads out from the South Shore trailhead, which is also the starting point for many of the other hikes in the area, such as Aster Falls, Aster Park, and Paradise Point. Unless you have teenagers who are aggressive hikers, you won't be able to see all these points plus Rockwell Falls on the same trip. Even if you can do the mileage, it's hard to enjoy each spot fully when doing them all together. We visited Aster Falls, Aster Park, and Paradise Point on one trip and then headed to Rockwell Falls on another day. Taking the boat *Sinopah*, operated by the Glacier Park Boat Company (see Resources), to the upper end of Two Medicine Lake provides a different access point for Rockwell Falls, so you aren't re-hiking so much of the South Shore Trail. From the boat landing we hiked to various locations (Upper Two Medicine Lake, Twin Falls, and No Name Lake), including Rockwell Falls. We got to see new terrain and enjoy a boat ride.

From the west end of the lake, begin down the only trail, leading to the left of the shelter. Hike just a few hundred yards to the first junction in the trail, where you take a hard left turn to head back along the south shore of the lake (a right turn leads you to a primitive toilet just a short distance down the trail). After rounding the end of the lake, you come out of the trees and begin to climb steadily for nice views down to the lake and probably of the *Sinopah* returning to the east-end dock. This section of the trail is the hardest thanks to the steady incline, but your legs should be fresh and the views distract you.

After about 1.5 miles the trail bends south, away from the lake and back into the trees, and the incline grows. If your children are tiring, encourage them: they are almost done with the uphill section and a snack spot lies just ahead. In about 0.5 mile you reach a signed crossroads. The left fork takes you back toward the Two Medicine Lake Campground. The right fork is marked "Cobalt Lake," which is the direction you need to go; Cobalt Lake is beyond Rockwell Falls along the way to Two Medicine Pass.

The next part of the trail leads among the trees on a meandering path with little elevation gain for about one more mile to your destination. As you approach the area surrounding the

Rockwell Falls make a great backdrop for a portrait.

base of the falls, you will see a few trail branches. Pass the first spur trail on your right (you can see the falls at this point) to head to the base of the falls. Though there is no "beach" area at the base, there are places to sit and relish the view.

You may be pleasantly surprised as you take in these falls and the many levels of cascades above, some of which you might not notice at first. Even as you sit in awe of the many tiers of falls that you can see, there are many more you that you cannot see from this vantage point. Herein lays the great fun of these particular cascades—exploring the many pools and drops above!

If you are visiting this spot with older, confident kids, now is a great time to let them climb and discover. Please remember that there is some risk of slipping, falling—and even drowning (some of the pools are deep)—when exploring areas like these. You are a substantial distance from emergency services, making any injury even more serious. Make sure everyone wears hiking shoes with good tread and "grippy" soles to navigate the rocks covered with gravel. Do not try to climb to the upper falls while wearing flip-flops or smooth-soled shoes! Evaluate your children's abilities and your own knowledge and preparedness for backcountry emergencies, and only allow them to explore this area to the degree you think best. If you are comfortable giving them the freedom to explore, they will be in for an amazing afternoon.

To reach the upper falls, use a fallen log to cross the pool at the base of the falls. From there, scramble up the rocks to the right of the main falls. If there is no log, walk back along the trail to the first spur and strike out uphill from there. This spur trail is mostly a social trail and has several small branches leading from it to another pool and drop area of the falls. There are almost too many of these areas to count!

Each one we visited had a wonderful flat area to sit and take in the waterfalls and the views. Each one had its own character, showing beautiful evidence of the carving of water on rock, revealing colorful striations and patterns that seemed to illuminate movement in the very rock itself.

Also, the higher up you go, the better the mountain views. Some spots reminded us of infinity pools, with the smooth clear water pooling up and disappearing over the rock of the cliff edge, as water, seemingly without boundary, frames the stunning views beyond.

The urge to swim in some of these pools may prove irresistible, particularly on a hot day. Many times it is dangerous to swim above a waterfall, but the deep pools and restricted openings help make these pools safe to wade and swim in. However, the water is bone-numbingly cold! If you do want to swim, be sure to bring a towel. You will want dry feet and dry clothes to hike out in.

We visited Rockwell Falls on a summer weekend, and a "free park admission" weekend at that (an option worth investigating; check out the NPS website). We encountered one family on the trail, and they were headed out. In the few hours we spent at the falls, we saw only one other group. Even on busier days, you can find privacy. Scramble up to a higher falls and sit by a pool—the steep nature of the rocks shields you from people below, and the sound of the waterfalls drowns out the sounds of others. The longer distance and the secluded nature of these falls make them an ideal destination if you are seeking adventure and solitude.

For the return trip, you have two options. If you took the boat out, you can ride back: your ticket is round-trip. Make sure you know the schedule, retrace your route to the dock, and don't miss the last boat! If you want to hike back, however, retrace your steps only as far as the crossroads, and take the now right-hand (east) fork; it eventually becomes the trail past Aster Park. You will end up at the South Shore trailhead and parking area. Taking the boat both ways shaves 1.3 miles of hiking in each direction, and the boat does add a dimension that you don't often get when hiking. Our recommendation is to get the boat ticket and enjoy both the ride and the hike!

Upper Two Medicine Lake

A gently rolling trail to a pristine backcountry lake, this hike incorporates a boat ride along the main Two Medicine Lake. While Upper Two Medicine Lake lacks the cobalt-blue waters of a glacier-fed lake, it is wild and beautiful all the same.

Distance: 4.4 miles out and back from the west-end boat dock, with 350 feet of elevation gain

Time: 2–3 hours

Starting point: West-side boat dock on Two Medicine Lake. (If your family wants more, this hike is made longer—10 miles round-trip—by starting from the North Shore trailhead in the campground at the north end of Pray Lake. We describe only the shorter route from the boat dock at the top of the lake.)

Disembark from the *Sinopah* and exit the boat dock to find the trail leading to the left of the shelter. You quickly reach the first junction with the South Shore Trail; continue straight ahead. If you are in need of a toilet, there is an outhouse to the left just a short way down the trail. (Take care that you don't end up going down the South Shore Trail—a hard left—in your pursuit of the outhouse.) After attending to your business, continue on the main trail, following signs to Upper Two Medicine Lake at the next junction, 0.7 mile ahead. (The signed branch to the right at this junction goes to Twin Falls.) Your mellow trail rolls along alternating between open and treed areas. Our four-year-old insisted on walking and was able to walk the whole way from the boat dock, so you know the trail is not too challenging. The views here are mostly up to the surrounding cliff-faced mountains, and they are beautiful. We saw a few mountain goats on these faraway cliffs; you'll appreciate having binoculars on this adventure.

Nearing the lake, you come over a small rise to see a smaller lake to the left below you. This is not your destination. Continue

The route to Upper Two Medicine Lake leads through rolling hills with low brush and great views.

past this lake and over the next hump, and get a first glimpse of Upper Two Medicine Lake ahead.

As you near Upper Two Medicine Lake, the trail fragments and can be hard to follow. This is because the main trail leads directly into the backcountry campground on the shores of the lake. A paper sign stapled to a post shows the location of each individual campsite, but there doesn't appear to be a "main" trail at this point. Just wind your way through the campground and toward the water, being respectful of campers. A big logjam at the lower end of the lake near you is a dangerous area, and kids should not be allowed to climb around on the logs, as they are often partially floating and can be very unstable. Instead, make your way along the shore, heading to your right, and find a place to relax and enjoy a nourishing snack while the kids throw pebbles in the water and float (and sink) stick boats.

After resting, head back the way you came and, if energy remains, be sure to add a side trip to Twin Falls (see below) on your way to the boat dock. Remember to get a copy of the boat schedule and be back before the last boat leaves, or you will have a long walk ahead of you! Finally, both lakes see quite a lot of wind, so bring protective clothing, like windbreakers, even on a warm day.

 Twin Falls

Twin Falls offers a short, easy hike that wanders through mature forest to an unusual and beautiful configuration of waterfalls. It has two bridge crossings and a well-defined trail, making it a good option even for families with very young children. With older children, combine it with the hike to Two Medicine Lake (above).

Distance: Just over 2 miles round-trip from the boat landing, with minimal elevation gain
Time: 1 hour
Starting point: West-end boat dock on Two Medicine Lake

Leaving the boat landing, you arrive almost immediately at the first junction with the South Shore Trail coming in from your left; keep going straight. At 0.7 mile you reach the junction with the North Shore Trail coming in from your right; again, continue straight toward Upper Two Medicine Lake. Soon you come to a second bridge crossing. This is your clue that you are getting close to the trail you want: the Twin Falls spur trail that comes in from the right. Don't worry about missing the turn; all the junctions are well marked, and the hiking is pleasant as you amble through a shady area of ferns, huckleberries, and thimbleberries.

The falls are beautiful, and the landscape around here provides plenty of opportunities for climbing, playing in the creek, exploring, and relaxing with a snack. Spend as much time as you like, and, if you are feeling up to it, hike 1.3 miles farther to Upper Two Medicine Lake (see above).

Leave time for exploring at Twin Falls.

No Name Lake

It may lack a name, but the lake at the end of the trail isn't short on charm. And the hike itself offers the lure of possible wildlife sightings and wildflowers. So why not take this relatively short, steep climb up a side canyon to a pretty little lake nestled in the trees at the base of a steep rock wall? While there's a bit of ascent, you're rewarded with views along the way and a sweet picnic spot on a pocket beach.

Distance: 5.4 miles round-trip, 905 feet of elevation gain
Time: 3–5 hours
Starting point: West-end boat dock on Two Medicine Lake

The trail leaves the boat dock from the west shore and winds through a broad forested valley with little elevation gain for almost a mile. At 0.7 mile you reach an intersection. Left leads to Twin Falls and Upper Two Medicine Lake (see above); for No Name Lake you want to head right (northeast). You soon start gaining a little elevation. Shortly after leaving the valley floor (0.4 mile), you reach another junction, this time with Dawson Pass Trail, which heads right and back along the north shore of the main Two Medicine Lake. Turn left instead, and travel west. The next 1.5 miles are the most challenging of the hike; the route steadily climbs, but it also offers wonderful views back over the valley from which you came.

On this section the forest thins, so there is more sun exposure and only occasional shade as you climb. (Be sure you've applied plenty of sunblock.) The clearings mean more flowers and better opportunities to see wildlife. Keep your eyes peeled for moose among the trees and mountain goats on the impossibly steep cliff faces of the surrounding mountains: we saw both. Ahead of you is a sharply pointed mountain jutting up through the trees on the horizon; it is known as Pumpelly Pillar, named after the leader of a railroad survey party that crossed Pitamaken Pass in 1883.

As you near the pillar, the trail climbs steeply through a series of short switchbacks, then once again enters a thick forest as you top out over the main ridge. The worst of the climbing is now behind you, and you are rewarded with some shade and rolling terrain of moderate ups and downs until you reach the junction with the No Name Lake Trail. From this intersection, it is a short 0.2 mile through abundant huckleberries to the head of the lake.

You soon see the lake and walk along its shores; the temptation to stop early is strong, but continue on. In a very short while you reach the backcountry campground that offers three campsites and a pit toilet and, even better, lake access with a small beach that makes a wonderful spot to take in the surrounding scenery and enjoy a refreshing snack. Once you have rested and finished your lake appreciation, turn around and retrace your steps back to the boat dock.

Panoramic views are the reward for making the ascent en route to No Name Lake.

Adventures Beyond Hiking

Being off the beaten path, Two Medicine offers fewer options than other regions of the park. You won't see horses on these trails, and it's not a great place to bike, aside from around the campground. Even tour buses are scarce; all of which might just be another reason we love this region!

Boating

As in the rest of the park, in the Two Medicine Region the Glacier Park Boat Company is the authorized provider of anything boat related. They offer a guided boat tour of Two Medicine Lake aboard their historic vessel, the *Sinopah*. This boat takes you on a cruise to the west end of the lake, where you can choose to get off and hike in some of the areas beyond that end of the lake or return on the boat. This boat tour is one of their best-priced options in Glacier and gives families who want to put in fewer trail miles access to some wonderful hiking above

The *Sinopah* awaits passengers on Two Medicine Lake. (NPS/David Restivo photo)

the lake. Not all kids are thrilled with an out-and-back boat tour, but most will welcome the chance to get off and hike above Two Medicine Lake and save their feet some miles.

You can also choose to rent canoes, one-or two-person kayaks, or rowboats. Although more expensive than the tour boat, small craft give you independence and the chance to paddle out on your own in the peaceful waters and experience tranquility of a different sort than found while hiking. Be aware of the current and predicted weather for the day, so that you don't find yourself out on the lake when a storm comes up.

Tour or self-propelled, boating is a fun way to let your kids experience another level of interaction with nature. We highly recommend either option, especially in this part of the park. We found Glacier Park Boat Company to be gracious and very flexible, especially when they happily moved a reservation to another region for us when forest fires meant we couldn't hike above the lake one summer. See Resources to find out more.

Tour Bus

There is no free park shuttle in the Two Medicine region. Your options are to take a Red Bus tour starting at the Many Glacier Hotel, the St. Mary Lodge (just outside the park entrance in the town of St. Mary), or the Rising Sun Motor Inn. Alternatively, Sun Tours buses leave from just outside the region in the towns of Browning and East Glacier. Read more about these options in the Planning Your Glacier Family Vacation chapter or online at their websites (see Resources).

Services and Amenities

Before Going-to-the-Sun Road opened in 1933, visitors on the east side of the park flocked to the Two Medicine Region. Now with the larger road open to the north, this region gets less attention, making it feel small and tucked out of the way. There are fewer lodging options and also fewer services in general. The people we've met in this area like it that way. They come here to get away from the crowds and the commercialism they see in other areas of the park.

There is a camp store located off the parking lot at the lake in a historic chalet (no longer offering lodging). Here you will find camp food, gifts, and park maps and books for sale. Porch benches directly outside the store are a nice way to get out of the rain on a less-than-ideal weather day. Also in the parking lot area is a small kiosk where you can rent a canoe, kayak, double kayak, or rowboat or purchase lake tours by boat from the Glacier Park Boat Company (see Resources).

There is no visitor center in this area. A small ranger station located just outside the Two Medicine Campground is staffed during limited hours on regular business days. The ranger station offers information on trail closures, animal sightings, trail maps, backcountry trips, and more.

The nearest major services outside the park are 11 miles away in East Glacier. There you can find gas, groceries, restaurants, and lodging.

WATERTON

A unique feature of Glacier National Park is its association with a partner park in Canada, Waterton National Park. UNSECO recognizes that boundaries between countries are artificial constructions and that the flora and fauna of this region have no understanding of boundaries. Therefore, they designated Glacier National Park–Waterton National Park, a World Heritage Site, as the first International Peace Park. This wonderful joining allows animals to follow their traditional migration paths.

Like Glacier, Waterton National Park encompasses a critical range of habitats, from plains to soaring mountains and all the water features in between. You will find many of the same geologic wonders in Waterton as you do in Glacier.

If you are interested in visiting, Waterton National Park is most easily accessed from the east side from a highway that heads north out of Great Falls, Montana, before crossing the international border. Keep in mind that in order to visit Waterton from Glacier, you will need all the documentation for crossing an international border as you would anywhere else. Be sure to check the current requirements at the time of travel, and remember that getting a passport book or card can take months and plan accordingly.

Waterton Glacier International Peace Park at the Chief Mountain Border Crossing (Martin Kraft / wikicommons photo)

Backcountry overnight camping allows for plenty of downtime and relaxation.

YOUR FIRST GLACIER BACKPACKING TRIP

With an overnight backpack trip at Glacier, your family can enjoy a true wilderness adventure that gets to the heart of some of the best things the park has to offer. While the thought of strapping everything on your back that you and your kids might need for a couple of nights of sleeping outside may seem overwhelming, the challenge is so worth it. If you honestly evaluate your skills and the abilities of the weakest (or most vulnerable) member and decide everyone is up for it and plan well, you will experience awesome rewards. Backpacking in Glacier can be daunting, what with the presence of bears, the variable weather, and the process involved in choosing a site and securing a permit. But if you follow certain precautions (see our section on bear safety), do your homework, choose your routes wisely, and plan your trip far enough in advance, all of those concerns can be easily addressed. This chapter tells you what you need to know and suggests three trip options suitable for kids.

There are 220 backcountry campsites in Glacier: sites that you have to walk to, not drive to, and that you need a permit to stay in. Half of the sites can be reserved months in advance by using an online application, while others can only be reserved in person within 48 hours of your trip. All the trips we recommend have campsites that can be reserved well in advance. Plan to submit your application by the appropriate deadline in March: March 1 for groups of nine to twelve and March 15 for groups of one to eight. All permit applications received by the appropriate deadline will be considered by the park on a first-come, first-served basis. (For backcountry application fees and more, see Resources for the Glacier National Park website.) If you are unsuccessful in drawing the trip you requested, you will be refunded part of the fee. There is an additional, per night fee that is payable when you pick up your permit, which you must do in person. Permits can be picked up at the St. Mary Visitor Center, Many Glacier Visitor Center, Two Medicine Ranger Station, Polebridge Ranger Station, and, in Alberta, Canada, at the Waterton Lakes National Park Visitor Centre.

If you want the backcountry experience without the sleeping-on-the-ground experience, check out the backcountry chalet option (see details in the "Backcountry Chalets" sidebar in the Glacier Camping and Lodging chapter). The chalet will even facilitate horse packing in your gear so you can avoid carrying everything yourself.

Before you fully commit to a backpacking trip, visit the Glacier National Park website (see Resources) to read Glacier Park regulations and watch a video on safety. The website also has a step-by-step tutorial walking you through the permitting process.

Now that you have some information to get you started, let us share some of the backpacking options at Glacier we think are ideal for doing with kids. When choosing a backpacking trip, we look for approaches that are short (around 4 miles or less), very little elevation gain (approximately 1000 feet or less), and that have a feature that kids will enjoy (like water). The following trip suggestions meet these criteria.

 Cobalt Lake

Traveling by boat across Two Medicine Lake cuts down the walking miles to this beautiful lake, but it's still a long, somewhat strenuous hike so we recommend this backcountry hike for families with older kids. Waterfalls on the walk in offer some distraction, but for maximum enjoyment, get to the campsite early and plan to explore after you've pitched your tent.

This small pool may soothe your feet on the trail to Cobalt Lake.

Distance: 4.5 miles each way from the boat landing, with 1400 feet of elevation gain
Time: 3–4 hours each way
Starting point: West-end boat dock on Two Medicine Lake
Campground code: COB
Campsite details: There are two sites here; both can be reserved ahead of time. The first date for which they can be reserved is August 1; the maximum stay in July, August, and September is one night. Wood fires prohibited.

Cobalt Lake lies farther along the trail to Rockwell Falls (see above), so if you've taken that hike, the route will look familiar. From the west end of Two Medicine Lake, where the boat drops you off, begin down the only trail, leading to the left of the shelter. After just a few hundred yards, you reach the first trail junction; take a hard left turn to head back along the south shore of the lake (a right turn leads you to a primitive toilet just a short distance down the trail). Round the lake to come out of the trees and begin to climb steadily, with views down to the lake.

After about 1.5 miles the trail bends south, away from the lake and back into the trees, and the incline grows; you reach a signed crossroads roughly 0.5 mile farther along the trail. The left fork takes you back toward the Two Medicine Lake Campground; you want the right fork that is marked "Cobalt Lake." In about 3.5 miles from the junction, you reach Cobalt Lake, having passed Rockwell Falls en route. Stop for a snack and a rest as needed on the hike in, but be sure you get to the campsite early enough to set up and settle in; you can backtrack to Rockwell Falls the next day, after breaking camp, to give your kids maximum time at the falls.

 No Name Lake

With a relatively short approach hike, thanks to the boat trip, No Name Lake is an ideal backcountry outing with opportunities for wildlife sightings and to explore farther afield.

No Name Lake is even nicer when you can linger longer.

Distance: 2.7 miles each way when using the Glacier Park Boat Company boat *Sinopah*, 905 feet of elevation gain
Time: 1–2.5 hours each way
Starting point: Boat dock on Two Medicine Lake by the South Shore trailhead
Campground code: NON
Campsite details: There are three campsites here, two can be reserved ahead of time. The first date for which they can be reserved is July 15; the maximum stay is one night. Wood fires prohibited.

The trail leaves the boat dock from the west shore and winds through a broad forested valley with little elevation gain for almost a mile. At 0.7 mile you reach an intersection. Left leads to Twin Falls and Upper Two Medicine Lake; for No Name Lake you want to head right (northeast). You start gaining a little elevation and soon (0.4 mile) you reach another junction, this time with Dawson Pass Trail, which heads right, and back along the north shore of the main Two Medicine Lake. Turn left instead and travel west. The next 1.5 miles are the most challenging of the hike; the route steadily climbs, but it also offers wonderful views back over the valley from which you came.

On this section the forest thins, so there is more sun exposure and only occasional shade as you climb. (Be sure you've applied plenty of sunblock.) The clearings mean more flowers and better opportunities to see wildlife. Ahead of you is a sharply pointed mountain jutting up through the trees on the horizon; it is known as Pumpelly Pillar, named after the leader of a railroad survey party that crossed Pitamaken Pass in 1883.

As you near the pillar, the trail climbs steeply through a series of short switchbacks, then once again enters a thick forest as you top out over the main ridge. The worst of the climbing is now behind you, and you are rewarded with some shade and rolling terrain of moderate ups and downs until you reach the junction with the No Name Lake Trail. From this intersection, it is a short 0.2 mile through abundant huckleberries to the head of the lake. You're nearly there; just a very short distance farther and you've reached your home for the night!

Overnighting at the lake increases your chance of seeing wildlife including mountain goats, moose, and bear. Since the campground is nestled against the flanks of Pumpelly Pillar, it is less subject to wind. From camp, it is a 2.2-mile climb each way to Dawson Pass, which provides a nice option for a day hike if you spend a full day in camp.

 Upper Two Medicine Lake

Minimal elevation gain and just over two miles each way, this makes a fairly easy backpacking trip for first timers or families with younger children, while day-trip options keep it interesting for older kids.

A logjam makes for a dangerous obstacle to dipping your feet in icy Upper Two Medicine Lake, but there is easier access farther along the shore.

Distance: 4.4 miles out and back, with 350 feet of elevation gain, when using the Glacier Park Boat Company boat *Sinopah*

Time: 2–3 hours each way

Starting point: Boat dock on Two Medicine Lake by the South Shore trailhead

Campground code: UPT

Campground details: There are four sites here, two of which can be reserved in advance. The first date they can be reserved for is July 15. The maximum stay is one night. Wood fires are not allowed.

From the boat dock, find the trail leading to the left of the shelter and quickly reach the first junction with the South Shore Trail; your route continues straight ahead, following the signs to Upper Two Medicine Lake at the next junction, 0.7 mile ahead. The trail is so gentle that even our four-year-old insisted on walking it. Your route takes you over a few small rises and around a smaller lake, after which you get your first view of Upper Two Medicine

Lake. The main trail leads directly into the backcountry campground on the shores of the lake.

Overnighting at the lake increases your chance of seeing wildlife such as moose and bear, and binoculars will reveal mountain goats high in the surrounding cliffs. There are also good day-hiking options nearby, including No Name Lake and Twin Falls, although they will likely see moderate traffic from day visitors who may also use the boat system to access the more remote areas.

THE BIG OUTSIDE

There is one additional resource we want to share with you to help you in your planning. We used Mike Lanza's "The Big Outside" website for much of our backpacking trip planning (see Resources). A note of caution: Not all of the articles there are aimed specifically at taking kids into the backcountry. We looked through the information for trips we felt our kids (and the adults carrying the extra gear) were up for and then made sure to implement strategies also shared on our website (see Resources), to help keep the kids going.

Mike evaluates trips he has taken with his kids and includes a lot of great information on backpacking or hiking with kids and in general. Their trip to the Lake Ellen Wilson backcountry campground (code ELL) is also worth checking out. His photography is "eye-candy" and will really get you excited to start planning your own family trip.

Spending the night in a tent can allow you to relax around a campfire.

CAMPING AND LODGING

Most of the campgrounds in Glacier National Park are first come, first served, but a few give you the opportunity to reserve your spot ahead of time. By "ahead of time" we mean as much as six months! This is a popular park. If you are planning on reserving camping or lodging, you should plan your trip well ahead of the time reservations are accepted and make sure you know when that time is. Be ready on the morning of the opening date and get online right away. Also, it is helpful to have a few options that will work for you, in case your first choice doesn't pan out. For options beyond camping, you will find historic grand hotels, cozy cabins, comfortable motels, and even a back-country chalet! Keep in mind that most of the lodging options were built long ago, imbuing them with lots of historic charm but also leaving them on the "rustic" side. When considering indoor lodging, you should assume the accommodations will be without TV, air conditioning, and Wi-Fi. If any of those are absolutely essential to you, discuss their availability with the reservation agent before you book. Out of so many options, we are sure you will find the right fit for your family.

QUICK TIPS FOR CAMPGROUNDS

We always spend our first night in the park with a reservation at a campground or lodge; that way we don't feel anxious wondering if we will get a spot as we are traveling to the park.

If you are going for a first-come, first-served campground, get there early in the day for the best chance at scoring a spot. The day before you go, check the National Park Service website's campground status page. One thing we love about Glacier National Park's website is the feature that allows you to see what time each campground filled in the last month. It's important to look at the last few days but also to look at the same day of the week for the last month. For example, if you are arriving on a Tuesday, look at the three previous Tuesdays to see when they filled. This gives you a general guideline for how early the campground fills on that particular day of the week. Looking at the last few days helps you see where you are in the season (things fill much sooner during the busier months). All this information is available at the park's website (see Resources). Go to "plan my visit" then "eating and sleeping." Scroll down to find the "camping page" link that will take you to a general information page. Find the link for "campground status." This will take you to a map and chart of all the campgrounds. You should be able to see information about when the campground filled "yesterday" and "today." If you click on the name of your campground, it will take you to a page with much more detail, including a calendar listing all of the fill times for that month.

If this seems too complicated, most visitor centers and even some entrances either post this information or will tell you if you call and ask. We use this information when we are already at the park camping and want to move to another campground that cannot be reserved in advance. It helps us know how early we need to get up and get moving in order to have a good chance of getting a site elsewhere.

Most campgrounds offer ranger programs throughout the day, where a park service naturalist will give a talk about some of the unique features of the park. The park-wide schedule for these is listed in the newspaper that you can pick up at the entrance or at any visitor center. However, the programs that are specific to your campground will usually be posted at the check-in station and often at the bathrooms. The talks are almost always informative and interesting, so check the lists to see if there is one that fits for your family.

One final note on camping in Glacier National Park: The park service reserves the right to cancel any tent site reservations due to animal activity (usually bears) in the area. They can do this even at the last minute. (They did this to us once. Fortunately, we live close enough that it wasn't disastrous, but it did mean we didn't make it to the park that fall.) Camping in bear country requires specialized attention to detail that may not be for everyone (see the Safety in the Park chapter). That, coupled with the risk of having your camping reservation canceled, may mean that a lodging option or hard-sided camper is best for your family. Read through the options below and choose something that will match your comfort and safety tolerances. We always camp in a tent, so we can vouch that tent camping is certainly possible, even with young kids.

LAKE MCDONALD REGION

The Lake McDonald Region boasts many options for camping and lodging. This book groups the resources at Apgar with those at Lake McDonald Lodge. Here you will find four lodging and four camping options. We'll consider the campgrounds first.

A typical campsite at Fish Creek Campground

Camping

The campgrounds located in this region are Fish Creek, Apgar, Sprague Creek, and Avalanche. Advance reservations are available only at Fish Creek and for half of the Apgar group sites (up to six months in advance for the individual sites and twelve months for the group sites). The others are first come, first served. Make your reservations at Recreation.gov.

Fish Creek

The Fish Creek Campground is located around the southwestern end of Lake McDonald, which is on the opposite end of the lake from most of the main attractions in this region. It is, however, very close to services and attractions in the Apgar

Glacier Campgrounds

CAMPGROUND	DATES	SITES	GROUP SITES
Lake McDonald Region			
Apgar	Late Apr–Early Oct*	192	10
Avalanche	Mid-June–Mid-Sept	87	
Fish Creek	Early June–Early Sept	180	
Sprague Creek	Early May–Mid-Sept	25	
St. Mary and Logan Pass Region			
Rising Sun	Early June–Mid-Sept	84	
St. Mary	Mid-Apr–Late Oct*	148	1
Many Glacier Region			
Many Glacier	Mid-May–Late Sept*	110	1
Two Medicine Region			
Two Medicine	Late May–Late Sept*	100	1

Note: Campgrounds marked with an * offer primitive camping outside the dates listed area and the drive to the northeastern-side services is not bad either. Even though it is the second largest campground in the park (after Apgar), Fish Creek sees little through traffic, since the road heading north of the campground (Inside North Fork Road) quickly becomes gravel and then primitive. There are many shaded and private campsites, and you can walk out of the campground and onto the Rocky Point and West Shore trails. An amphitheater offers a variety of ranger-led programs. There are also showers in loop A that are for registered campers only. We have enjoyed stays here because there are easy trails leaving directly from the campground that lead to bridges over creeks and beaches along the lake, all well suited to kids, with plenty of the things that catch their interest.

LUSH OILETS	DISPOSAL STATION	NOTES
•	•	25 sites with space for 40' campers
•		50 sites with space for 26' campers
•	•	18 sites with space for 35' campers, and 62 with space for 27' campers
•		Some sites have space for 21' campers
•	•	10 sites with space for 25' campers
•	•	3 sites for 40' campers, and 22 sites with space for 35' campers
•	•	13 sites with space for 35' campers
•	•	10 sites with space for 35' campers

Apgar

With 192 sites, this campground is the largest in Glacier and offers access to many services, including those found in the Apgar Village (gift shops, camp store, and a reservation station for boat rentals, horseback riding, and tour buses), the park's free shuttle service, and the Apgar Visitor Center. There is an amphitheater for evening programs and many ranger-led activities, which you will find listed on bulletin boards around the campground. There are also kid-friendly trails and even bike paths in the area close by.

Sprague Creek

Sprague Creek Campground is tucked neatly between Going-to-the-Sun Road and Lake McDonald. It has 25 sites with no RV access. Tent campers looking for a quiet campground might be disappointed by the road noise but will not have to endure generators running, and the free shuttle makes a stop here for easy access to other points along Going-to-the-Sun Road. There are many shaded sites, some directly on the shores of Lake McDonald. While these are fabulous scenic sites, and the

There are some mighty fine views at Sprague Creek Campground.

shuttle access is convenient, parents need to be advised that the location may not be very safe for small children, what with the road on one side and the lake on the other.

Avalanche

Situated near gorgeous and popular hiking options, Avalanche Lake and the Trail of the Cedars, this campground has 87 sites, most of which are shaded from the sun in the summer months. There is an amphitheater a short walk away that offers interesting ranger-led evening programs on topics including, but not limited to, history, the starry night skies, and animals in the area. Each ranger chooses a topic they are excited to share and creates a presentation for their program. Their passion often comes through and is catching! There is also a stop here for the free shuttle service along Going-to-the-Sun Road.

Lodges, Inns, and Motels

Maybe you are just not the camping type or are more concerned about bears or weather in this particular park: do not worry! In the indoor-sleeping category there are many excellent options available to choose from. The summaries below will assist you in choosing the best option for your family.

Apgar Village Lodge & Cabins

Apgar Village lies just inside the west entrance to the park and is close to the main park activities taking place at the Apgar Visitor Center. The area around this lodge seems a little more commercialized and perhaps a bit run down. That said, the motel rooms are reasonably priced for national park lodging, and the cabins are a good option for families. They have fully outfitted kitchens, allowing you to save some money by preparing your own food.

The Apgar Village accommodations are run by a company called Glacier Park, Inc. (see Resources). We found it somewhat difficult to get information from their website. You must first enter your dates on the Glacier Park, Inc. site and then choose your accommodation type from a drop-down menu. Once you submit this information, the website will let you see the available dates calendar—at which time you may need to adjust your dates to match availability and then hit "search" again. Finally, you will see a price. This isn't your total cost however! You will need to click on "More Room and Pricing Details" before you see the actual amount you will pay. This is a tedious way to search, but it's their system.

Village Inn at Apgar

Although it lacks some of the old-world grandeur (having been built in 1956 instead of at the turn of the twentieth century), the Village Inn still has much to offer. The inn offers many units with kitchens, so if you are hoping to sleep indoors and still save money by preparing your own food, this is a good option. There are also standard motel rooms, family units that sleep five to six, and a few ADA-accessible rooms.

The inn is located on the shores of Lake McDonald (literally on the shore) just 2 miles from the park's west entrance. Every room has fantastic views of the water and mountains beyond.

The Village Inn in Apgar Village has its own mid-century modern charm. (NPS/David Restivo photo)

There are no other amenities in the immediate area, but dining and tours are available just 8 miles away in the area around the Lake McDonald Lodge. Book your stay through Glacier National Park Lodges (Xanterra Parks & Resorts—see Resources), a much easier website to navigate than that of Glacier Park, Inc.

Lake McDonald Lodge, Cabins & Suites

This is the historic, turn-of-the-century, Swiss-style lodge that you expect to see in the great parks. Built in 1913 on the shores of the lake, the Lake McDonald Lodge is a sight to see. The sleeping options here (82 rooms) are divided between the three-story lodge, a row of cabins, Snyder Hall, and the exquisite Cobb House. These accommodations are all located in a "village" that includes many food options, tour bookings and departure locations, and evening ranger programs.

The lodge rooms are spread over three floors, and each has a private bath. They were remodeled in 2015; despite the rustic look, they are quite up to modern standards. The cabin rooms are "duplex" with a shared wall but no door between the units. They have private bathrooms, also updated in 2015. The Cobb House boasts three suites, each with a sitting area, private bath, queen beds, sleeper sofas, and flat-screen TVs.

Snyder Hall is a renovated historic dormitory with eight hostel-style rooms with in-room sinks but a shared bathroom. The prices vary greatly, as you might expect; see Glacier National Park Lodges (Xanterra Parks & Resorts—see Resources).

If you will be taking a boat tour or a Red Bus tour, or enjoying an evening ranger program, you will find yourself in the grand historic lodge. It is a beautiful piece of park history, so take a moment to enjoy it. Although it is on the shores of the lake, the lobby/lounge area isn't very open to the water. There is a nice porch, however, out the back doors, which overlooks the water, and you'll discover many places to sit or wander, along with some pebbly beachfront. There are also bathrooms located in the lobby.

Lake McDonald Lodge is a classic Swiss-style lodge. (NPS/Jacob W. Frank photo)

The rehabilitated Cobb House (NPS photo)

Motel Lake McDonald

These two 1950s style motel buildings are located in the same area as the historic lodge. They are near the shores of the lake but lack lake views. The second-floor rooms are accessed by exterior stairs only. Every room has a private bathroom, and there are no connecting rooms. Book your stay through Glacier Park, Inc. (see Resources), but see our comments above under "Apgar Village Lodge & Cabins" for notes on using their frustrating website.

ST. MARY AND LOGAN PASS REGION

The St. Mary region serves as the main hub for activities on the east side of the park. Its east entrance is the closest access to Logan Pass, and many people approach Logan Pass from this side. This region has two campgrounds, one motor inn, and (near Logan Pass) a backcountry chalet.

Camping

In this popular region of the park, there are two campgrounds: St. Mary and Rising Sun. They are both located just off Going-to-the-Sun Road, and the free shuttle makes a stop near each. Make your reservations at Recreation.gov.

St. Mary Campground

The largest campground on the east side of the park, St. Mary has three loops and 148 sites. The campground is located just over the river from the St. Mary Visitor Center, where you can find interpretive programs and park information, as well as free shuttle pickup and drop-off stops. Just outside the park boundary, but only about 10 minutes away, is the town of St. Mary, where you will find gas, groceries, restaurants, and many other lodging options.

Although shade is generally sparse here, loop A provides a bit of shelter. This loop is also generator-free, making it a good option for families who are tent camping. Loops B and C are less sheltered, although a lot of thick low brush does provide some privacy between sites. The openness also leads to nice views of Singleshot, East Flattop, and Red Eagle mountains. There are flush toilets, water spigots (each shared by three or four sites), and, in loop C, showers for registered campers only.

The St. Mary Campground is open year-round, though with very limited services in the off-season (for example, the water is shut off to prevent the pipes from freezing). From early September through the end of May, all sites are first come, first served;

St Mary Campground offers some nice meadows for kids to explore.

reservation season begins at the start of June and runs through August. There is no fee to camp during the winter camping season, December 1 through March 31 (you you must still pay the park entrance fee, of course). Also, no water is available during the primitive winter season. For fees, reservations, or to learn more, visit Recreation.gov.

Rising Sun Campground

Rising Sun Campground is located 6.2 miles from the St. Mary Entrance station, about midway up St. Mary Lake. There are 84 sites with shared potable water spigots and flush toilets. Sites 49–84 are generator free. All sites are first come, first served.

Adjacent to the campground is a camp store, a casual restaurant, and token-operated showers (one stall for women, one for men). The free park shuttle has a stop here, and across the road and down toward the lake is one of the boat docks for boat tours of the lake. For fees or reservations, visit Recreation.gov.

Lodges, Inns, and Motels

If you don't plan to camp or stay at a chalet, your only lodging option in this region is the well-situated Rising Sun Motor Inn.

Rising Sun Motor Inn

The Rising Sun was built in 1940, and it is rustic but not grand like the old lodges. It offers individual cabins and motel rooms. The complex sits on a hill about a quarter of a mile from the shores of St. Mary Lake. Here you'll find a full-service restaurant, general store, gift shop, and stops for the Red Bus tours as well as the free shuttle bus to Logan Pass. Across Going-to-the-Sun Road is a boat dock for boat tours on St. Mary Lake.

The inn rooms are two types—some accessed from outside and some from an interior hallway off the general store. The duplex cabins share a wall between units. Each has a private bathroom. Cooking is not permitted in any of the units.

For reservations, photos, and more info, visit Glacier National Park Lodges (see Resources).

BACKCOUNTRY CHALETS

Fairly unusual when it comes to national park lodging, these distinctive backcountry chalets offer an experience you won't soon forget. In most national parks in the United States, the backcountry is open only to those willing and able to pack all of their food and gear on their backs, severely limiting the number of people who get to see the less populated areas of the park. For those who are willing and able, this is an essential wilderness experience. However, it leaves the majority of visitors on main roads and trail systems. The backcountry chalets at Glacier open up a small part of the backcountry to those who are willing to hike in, but don't want to carry a lot of gear. They also offer what most backcountry campers would consider to be luxury accommodations and delicious food without all the effort of carrying it all in on your back!

Granite Park Chalet

This backcountry chalet was built in 1914–1915. It is listed as a National Historic Landmark and is set in a breathtaking location. High in the mountains near the Continental Divide, it rests on a grassy knob surrounded by soaring peaks, ageless trees, and wildlife galore. It can be reached by hikers in three ways: via the Highline Trail near the Logan Pass Visitor Center (7.6 miles, 800 feet of elevation gain), from the Swiftcurrent trailhead at Many Glacier (7.6 miles, 2300 feet of elevation gain), and from the Loop trailhead off Going-to-the-Sun Road (4.2 miles, 2200 feet of elevation gain; see the hike, Granite Park from the Loop trailhead, described in the St. Mary and Logan Pass section of this book).

This chalet has some notable features. First, you are on your own for preparing meals, although if you wish to pre-order from their menu, the concessioner (see Resources) will have food items delivered to the chalet for you. For your use in preparing your own food, there is a kitchen building with a twelve-burner stove; a double oven; and a limited selection of pots, pans, and kitchen utensils. You must bring

Granite Park Chalet offers indoor accommodations in the backcountry.

your own personal flatware and dishes. Note that no water is available for your use at the chalet. The water source is a quarter of a mile away along a rocky, rugged trail, so you need to come prepared to haul it and treat it. On some occasions, water may be available to purchase in limited quantities. Bedding is not automatically provided. Many guests bring their own sleeping bag, while others choose to rent linens. The restroom is a modern pit toilet in a separate building.

This chalet is open from June 27 through September 10. The best way to make reservations is online and far in advance (see Resources); reservations open up in January and often fill within a week. The chalet can also be accessed on horseback. For information on riding to the chalet, check with Swan Mountain Outfitters (see Resources).

Sperry Chalet

Until recently Glacier National Park had two chalets, but in the summer of 2017 the Sperry Chalet burned in the Sprague Fire, and all the wooden portions of the structure were lost. However, the walls of the chalet were finely crafted out of native stone and remained standing, so as this book went to press, the Glacier Park Conservancy was starting a fundraising campaign to rebuild the beautiful structure, which was originally built in 1913. We don't yet know what will come of this effort and when, but if you are interested in learning more, check out the conservancy and concessionaire websites (see Resources) to learn the latest news. The information below gives you a sense of what the chalet offered before it was lost to fire.

Set in a stunning location high above Lake McDonald, this backcountry lodge was meant to impress. Although visitors slept indoors in private rooms, there was no power or heat. What water there was was found in cold water sinks in the restroom building or in the dining hall. Guests were not allowed to use candles or fueled lights, so they needed to bring a flashlight to use at night. The chalet did provide plenty of warm blankets!

Additionally, chalet staff provided three meals daily. Breakfast and dinner were served in the dining building, while lunch was either a sack lunch to take while day hiking or a la carte at the chalet. The a la carte lunch was also available to any day hikers, horseback riders, or backcountry campers who dropped in for lunch at Sperry; for breakfast or dinner, those not staying at the chalet had to make reservations in advance.

If the Sperry Chalet is reopened, it should be accessible from either the Lake McDonald Region via the Sperry trailhead (6.3 miles, with an elevation gain of 3423 feet, about 4.5 hours) or from the Jackson Glacier Viewpoint along Going-to-the-Sun Road between St. Mary and Logan Pass, along the Gunsight Pass trail (13.5 miles, with an elevation gain of 3300 feet, about 9 hours). If you opt to hike to the reopened (fingers crossed!) Sperry Chalet, you and your children will need to be in excellent shape, and even then we recommend the shorter route from Lake McDonald. If hiking that far isn't an option for your family, you might consider riding horses instead (for children age 7 and up only). Swan Mountain Outfitters (see Resources) is the concessioner for horseback rides in Glacier National Park. Note that before the fire, it wasn't an inexpensive experience and it's likely to be only pricier after the expense of rebuilding, but for the right occasion, it can be worth it.

MANY GLACIER REGION

This region of the park has one campground option and two hotel/lodge accommodations. It is also an access point for the Granite Park Chalet.

Camping

There's just one campground option for you in this region of the park.

Many Glacier Campground

The Many Glacier Campground is very popular but only half of its sites can be reserved in advance in the summer (June 15 through September 4). The rest of the sites are first come, first served during this period. In the shoulder seasons they are all first come, first served. The campground has 109 sites, some of which are on a generator-free loop. Just outside the campground there is a large parking area that is the access point for many area hikes. The Swiftcurrent Motor Inn, camp store, and a family-friendly restaurant are located on the far side of the parking lot. There is also a bathing house near the Swiftcurrent Motor Inn that has three showers for men, four for women, and one ADA-accessible shower stall. Showers are token operated. More resources are located just down the road at the historic Many Glacier Hotel, where you can make reservations for boat tours, horse tours, Red Bus tours, and Sun Tour services. The hotel also has interpretive programs, fine dining, and other entertainment that is often suitable for kids. If it is cold and rainy, and tent camping is wearing on your family, drop in at the hotel for hot chocolate from the small store in the lower level and enjoy the views from one of the comfortable lounging areas in the hotel lobby overlooking the lake.

Lodges, Inns, Motels and Chalets

Historically, the Many Glacier Region was a very active part of the park. Some evidence of this can be seen in the presence of

Many Glacier Hotel sits on the shore of Swiftcurrent Lake.

the stunning Many Glacier Hotel, which is one of three indoor sleeping options in the area, the others being a motel and cabins.

Many Glacier Hotel

The Many Glacier Hotel is one of the magnificent historic lodges in the national park system. Built by the Great Northern Railway in 1914–15, it is situated in the "American Alps" along the banks of the beautiful Swiftcurrent Lake, which means it takes in amazing lake and mountain views. There are standard rooms, suites, and family rooms, some with views of the lake. For booking and prices, see Xanterra Parks & Resorts in Resources.

The hotel is wonderful to visit even if you are not staying there. A grand lobby with many cozy reading nooks and furniture arranged for lounging is perfect for visiting with friends and family. The hotel is also where you will find the evening programs with park naturalists, the boat dock for cruises on the lake, and information and ticketing for Red Bus tours and horseback rides.

Swiftcurrent Motor Inn

Located close to the campground, the camp store, easygoing and family-friendly dining, and many of the region's trailheads, the Swiftcurrent Motor Inn is an excellent choice for lodging. The complex of inns and cabins includes motel-style units with external access; hotel-style rooms accessed by interior hallways; and heated cabins, with either a private bath or access to a bath and shower facility. For reservations and more information, contact Xanterra Parks & Resorts (see Resources).

Granite Park Chalet

This chalet is somewhat like a youth hostel in terms of amenities provided, but given its stunning location near the Continental Divide it might still seem like paradise once you arrive! There are multiple trail options to reach the chalet; see the more detailed description in the Backcountry Chalets sidebar.

TWO MEDICINE REGION

The Two Medicine Region is often thought of as the least developed of the developed areas of the park, which is of course one of the things many visitors, including our family, love about it. That being the case, there are fewer options here for places to stay. There are no grand lodges or even small hotels. If you come to Two Med, as it is affectionately called, you will need to camp.

Camping

There is just the one campground option in Two Med, but what a campground it is!

Two Medicine Campground

Our family loved this campground. It is tucked away along the shores of Pray Lake, which is a quiet and private setting. The water is shallow and the beach is covered with thousands of wonderful skipping rocks. You can walk easily from camp to the ranger station and even to Two Medicine Lake if you choose. There is also a large parking lot in the vicinity of Pray Lake.

This campground has three loops containing a total of 100 sites. Sites cannot be reserved ahead of time; every site is available on a first-come, first-served basis. Sites 1–36 are generator-free.

Two Medicine Campground offers a quiet place to play for your youngest campers.

A limited number of sites are able to accommodate long RVs. There are bathrooms with running water and flush toilets and shared potable water spigots between every two or three sites. The overnight fee can be paid at the self-serve box at the entrance to the campground (see Recreation.gov for fees and other information).

Here's an insider tip for getting a site here. There are a very limited number of ADA-accessible camping sites, located adjacent to the bathrooms. If you read the small print on the sign designating the site as wheelchair accessible, you will see that after 3:00 p.m., if the site isn't being used or already reserved by a person with a handicap, anyone can take it. If you have driven down here only to find all the sites taken, plan to be around and ready at 3:00 p.m. to claim the site. Go so far as getting a form from the kiosk and filling it out that morning, so you have it at the ready when a site opens up and is available to you; then put your stuff in the site and drop the envelope in the box. You just got your site in an otherwise full campground!

Where there are tasty treats like thimbleberries, there may also be bears.

SAFETY IN THE PARK

The utter wildness of Glacier National Park is one of its chief attractions but can also present risks. Bears and other wild animals, cold temperatures, swift water, and summer lightning storms should all be treated with respect. This chapter provides some guidelines to help keep you and your family safe.

STAYING SAFE IN BEAR COUNTRY

Bears are one of the first things people think about when planning a visit to Glacier. Glacier National Park has the highest density of grizzly bears in the Lower 48, which is exciting but also nervewracking for parents. But it's important to keep in mind that dangerous bear encounters are extremely rare. Glacier receives between two and three million visitors every year in the front- and backcountry, yet in the last fifty years has experienced only ten fatalities from bears. Knowing what to expect and how to behave in bear country brings the odds even more in your favor. Of the ten fatalities in half a century, only three involved hikers, and two of those were solo hikers—we doubt your kids will be hiking on their own.

On the other hand, there are typically one to two incidents a year where someone accidentally surprises a bear—quite often, a sow with a cub—and the female bear responds defensively and with aggression, an experience worth avoiding!

The presence of big wildlife, such as grizzly bears, is a good reason to follow practices designed to keep you safe. We address some of these below, but go to the National Park Service website to learn more about hiking and camping in grizzly bear and mountain lion country (see Resources).

Hang food and other smelly items between trees, not from a single tree that a bear could climb.

When Camping

Glacier National Park has a strict set of rules in place to deter bears, many of them revolving around preventing bears from associating humans with easy-to-reach backpacks full of food. Keeping food away from bears protects you; it also helps keep bears in the park wild—and alive. When you arrive at a campground—and even as you plan your trip—review the latest park requirements carefully; failing to follow them can result in a citation (or much worse, a negative bear interaction) and the recommendations do change from time to time.

The first rule in bear country is to store food properly. Unless you're actively preparing, consuming, or cleaning up after a meal, keep all food, even seemingly scent-free items, locked away in a rigid, lockable container. If you plan to backpack, several companies sell bear-proof containers authorized for park use; they're a great item to include on your family backcountry excursion. When camping in campgrounds accessible from the main road, your vehicle is an acceptable storage locker, as are the metal food lockers that the park service provides, one for every two or three campsites, at every campground in Glacier.

Remember that bears can pop open coolers. A number of high-end cooler companies have recently started selling coolers that are "certified bear proof," but these won't satisfy the park rangers. For one thing, it only has to look like a cooler to be an attractant to bears because they expect (rightly so) that it might contain food. Even if they can't get into these new and improved coolers, they still might spend a rowdy evening in your campsite trying. You really don't want that! Also remember: tents don't count as safe places to keep food, nor do the pop-up trailer tents that you tow behind your car. Both are useless against a hungry bear. When you think bear proof, you need to think of something that you could not penetrate with a sharp knife or hatchet.

Hanging food from a tree is no longer recommended, because many bears can climb, especially black bears. However, all of the backcountry sites provide either bear poles—where you can hang your food out of reach since bears can't climb a pole with no limbs—or bear lockers.

The next most important consideration is to keep a clean camp. You may have put your food in the car, but have you left crumbs all over the benches? Did you smear mayonnaise on the picnic table by accident, or cook hotdogs over the fire and spill the juice from the package on the ground near the campfire? Just think of the mess that s'mores can make. The thing is, bears have an incredibly powerful sense of smell (they can smell up to a mile away!) and so a good deal of care needs to be taken not to create a smelly mess. And yes, we have four kids, so we do understand

HOLE IN THE WALL
CAMPGROUND ⮕

NO STOCK ALLOWED BEYOND
THIS POINT

WARNING

BEAR
FREQUENTING AREA
Spur Trail, Campground
and Boulder Pass Trail

**There is no guarantee of your safety
while hiking or camping in bear country.**

Removal of this sign may result in injury to others
and is prohibited by law.

Some bear signs are less ambiguous than others. (NPS/David Restivo photo) what a challenge this can be. Try bringing a plastic tablecloth for mealtimes. That will often contain much of the mess and make cleanup a snap. Make sure all crumbs, bones, orange peels, and so forth are disposed of in a bear-proof garbage can.

You and the kids should not take smelly items into your tent at night. Things like toothpaste, skin lotion, and sunscreen have strong odors that can attract a bear, so you'll need to store those in the bear-proof locker as well. Even items that look like food containers but do not have smells are a concern. We typically carry a couple large jugs of water with us when we go camping, and one evening we left an empty one of these outside our car because water has no odor. The local campground host informed us that we needed to put it in our car as well, because bears can associate certain containers as having the appearance of food containers and may stop by to investigate. These campground rules are strict, but they have done a good job of keeping people and bears out of conflict. It's a smart idea to follow them.

When Hiking

The first precautions that you should take when hiking in bear country are simply to travel in a group and stay vigilant. A group of people is naturally seen as a stronger force to a wild animal than is a solitary person, so hiking in a group of people is one of the single most effective measures you can take to increase safety. Next comes being aware of your surroundings, because the sooner you can spot the bear, the less likely it is that things will escalate. It is the surprised bear that decides to lash out in defense, and a surprised bear is the main cause of most attacks.

When hiking, your two best friends are noise and bear spray. Bears are typically secretive creatures, and they really would prefer to avoid interactions with people, so by making noise you are providing them with advance warning of your approach and giving them time to move off. Fortunately, if you are traveling with kids, creating noise is seldom a problem! Simple conversations along the trail are a good start. Another recommendation is to occasionally clap your hands or say loudly and often, "hey, bear" as you round corners or approach areas with limited visibility such as thick undergrowth. Let them know you are coming. Some folks hang bells on their backpacks, and these are fine so far as they go, but the sound doesn't travel as far as voices do, and chimes can easily be drowned out by wind or the noise of a creek.

If all of these measures fail, and you do find yourself unexpectedly close to a bear, stay calm. Remember, bears aren't looking to confront you; they are very much looking to avoid you. Gather your family together to present a larger force to the bear, and never turn and run. Running spells "prey" to a bear, and you might trigger a predatory response. Instead, stay together and back away slowly. Keep facing the bear so you can judge its response to your presence, but avoid eye contact since that can be interpreted as aggression. Talk to your kids and others in your party in even, measured tones, so that you are keeping everyone calm and telling them what to do. Your voice alone tells the bear that you are human and not something else. Slowly increase the distance between you and the bear until you are at a safe distance before turning away.

In the unlikely event that a bear actually charges you, it is time to deploy the bear spray. Oh wait, is it buried in your backpack? Too bad, because it won't do you much good in there! Bear attacks happen in "surprise" situations, so by definition you won't have a long time to respond. When hiking, we always keep our bear spray where it can be accessed rapidly. It typically is sold with a holster that attaches to your belt, a good option. Consider hanging the holster from the chest strap that connects your two backpack shoulder straps, or storing it in a hip belt pocket or on a loop; less desirable, because harder to reach, is a side pocket on your backpack or day pack. Make sure you can grab the canister and remove it for action without having to take your pack off.

You will need to be fast on the draw, and you want to leave your backpack on for protection. If the bear keeps coming closer and you need to spray it, create a cloud of spray between you and the bear by aiming fairly low and using a sweeping motion back and forth as if you were painting a wall. The stream of spray is incredibly strong (about twice as strong as pepper spray for self-defense against humans), and once the bear gets a face-full it will change its mind quickly. A side note: Don't even think of spraying it on your tent or clothes as a deterrent—not only does this not work, it is not safe.

There is a good body of evidence that demonstrates that bear spray works to deter bear attacks. A 2012 study published in the *Journal of Wildlife Management* reviewed all bear attacks in North America going back to 1883. Since 1985 when bear spray was developed, there have been 83 encounters involving 156 people that have resulted in only 3 injuries, and none of them were fatal. That is a 98 percent success rate.

If you fail to get the spray out in time and the bear is on you, lie on your stomach to protect your vital areas and clasp your hands behind your head and neck. Your pack on your back is extra protection. Play dead so that you communicate to the bear that you are not a threat. Most attacks last only seconds until the bear realizes they or their cubs are safe, although it will seem much longer! It's important to run your kids through these drills and practice them for muscle memory, so that they know how to respond in the dreadful, unlikely event.

Learn as much as you can before you head for your Glacier adventures: the park service has an excellent web page dedicated to bear safety that provides lots of interesting detail, as well as an informative video (see Resources).

DEALING WITH THE WEATHER

Have you noticed the name of this park? It is probably not the warmest place that you will visit in summer. In fact, you can get snow in Glacier any month of the year, even if it doesn't always stick. You and the kids need to come prepared for every possible kind of weather, and that means dressing in layers and bringing adequate rain gear. Outfitting an entire family with good gear can get expensive, but you don't need to go overboard with everyone dressed like they just stepped out of the North Face catalog ready for an Everest expedition.

An inexpensive fleece jacket provides excellent insulation, but avoid anything cotton or cotton-mix, including hoodies and other sweatshirts. These may be fine for sweating in the gym, but when cotton gets wet it loses almost all of its insulation value. By contrast, clothing made of synthetic fiber and/or wool maintains its insulation value when wet from the sweat of exertion or an afternoon thunderstorm. Waterproof/breathable fabrics are most effective, although they come at a price, and the lighter in weight they are, the more expensive they get. These are especially important for long-distance backpackers, but for shorter adventures a simple nonbreathable waterproof shell costs a lot less and will still keep you dry during an unexpected rain shower, even if you get a bit clammy inside. Good gear increases your family's enjoyment, comfort, and safety while hiking, but you don't need to break the bank or be dissuaded from participating in the outdoors because you don't have all the latest trends in backcountry gear.

A couple of relatively inexpensive but necessary specialty items include a warm hat and wool socks. Hats are lightweight, easy to carry (take one, take two!) and go a long way toward keeping kids warm in a pinch, because a lot of heat is lost through the head and ears. Wool socks are soft and comfortable these days. You can find good deals online for merino wool socks, even in kid's sizes, and the finer gauge of this wool makes it non-itchy and even more effective as insulation. Wool also has natural odor-fighting properties—very handy—and wicks moisture away, helping to prevent blisters—a definite plus—especially for kids. We splurged on some for our family, and the kids love them. They have made the many miles we have hiked much more pleasant.

Check out the chart of average temperatures and temperature ranges for the months that you are most likely to visit the park. These numbers come from West Glacier at an elevation of

Glacier National Park Weather Averages

Month	Average High Temperature (F)	Average Low Temperature (F)	Average Precipitation Rain (inches)	Average Precipitation Snow (inches)
January	28	15	3.4	39.6
February	35	19	2.4	22.5
March	42	23	1.9	14.5
April	53	30	1.8	3.5
May	64	37	2.6	0.4
June	71	44	3.3	0.2
July	79	47	1.8	0
August	78	46	1.6	0
September	67	39	2.1	0.1
October	53	32	2.3	2
November	37	25	3.1	17.2
December	30	18	3.3	37.5

3200 feet. The eastern side of the park is typically higher and therefore a bit cooler as well. Furthermore, when you travel into the high-country areas, hundreds of feet higher, such as Logan Pass (at 6646 feet), it is very common for the temperature to be 10–20 degrees cooler and for it to be windier too. Always carry extra layers and be prepared for whatever might come your way.

Lightning

Thunderstorms are common in the Rocky Mountains and at Glacier. In addition to the cold and wet, they bring the danger of lightning strikes. When you or your kids spot dark clouds forming on the horizon, you need to think about finding shelter soon. You can tell how far away you are from a storm by counting: The speed of sound is approximately 340 meters per second depending on temperature and elevation. This equates to 1115 feet per second, or 0.21 miles per second. So if you see a lightning flash and count five seconds until you hear thunder, you are only one mile away from the lightning! But don't wait to find out. Move quickly as soon as you see the storm coming.

Stay alert to changes in weather even when you're distracted by amazing scenery.

Find cover fast by getting off of high points and finding a group of trees of moderate and equal height. Don't be the tallest thing out there, and don't stand under the tallest tree in the area as it may act like a lightning rod.

ELEVATION AND ALTITUDE SICKNESS

As you may remember from science class, the higher, you go the less dense the air is. That means that as you go higher, the air particles are more "spread out," and a normal breath of air will actually contain fewer air molecules and therefore less oxygen. If you live at lower elevations you will probably notice that you are breathing a little harder when exerting yourself at Glacier. Hikes might take a bit more time.

Most people can handle the change of altitude up to 8000 feet with little problem. But how will you know if one of your party isn't handling it well? They might start to feel a collection of flu-like symptoms including headache, nausea, fatigue, and dizziness. These typically start six to eight hours after ascending to altitude and generally subside in one to two days. Exertion exacerbates the problem. Returning to lower elevations is the quickest fix, and fortunately most of the camping and lodging areas in Glacier are in the lower regions.

DEHYDRATION

Cold, high mountain air also tends to be much lower in relative humidity—it is "dry" air. Breathing dry air into moist lungs causes you to lose water faster upon exhaling. What looks like altitude sickness (headache, nausea, fatigue, and dizziness) is often caused by dehydration, so make it a point for everyone in the family to drink more than usual during your Glacier visit to stay hydrated; you'll all feel better for it. It's often difficult to get younger children to drink enough fluids. You may not normally give your kids juices or flavored drinks, but when adventuring outdoors at altitude, choose hydration over concerns about sugary drinks. Those little tubes of individually sized drink mixes work well. Kids can choose a favorite flavor and add a tube to their water bottle. We also indulge in sports drinks for our kids while exerting ourselves in the outdoors.

FIRST-AID KITS

Carrying a simple first-aid kit is always a good idea, but this is especially true the farther you are from help. Having a first-aid kit in your car and on every hike and backpack trip brings peace of mind and could be life saving. Kits for your car are going to be larger, heavier, and more complete than those you carry with you. Those built for hiking need to be small and light enough that you will actually bring it with you when you go. (And if it isn't with you, it isn't of much use.) All outdoor retailers carry some type of first-aid kit; so do most pharmacies. Find one that works for you and your family and keep it handy.

You can also easily create your own kit. See Travel Checklists to read our recommended basics.

TRAVEL CHECKLISTS

WILDLIFE CHECKLIST

The following list includes animals commonly sighted in the park. Many more call the park home, but this list should keep your kids entertained and engaged. If you think you see an animal you can't identify, stop by a visitor center or talk with a ranger for help in identifying it.

Mammals

☐ Bats (many types)
☐ Bears (grizzly bear and black bear)
☐ Beaver
☐ Bighorn sheep
☐ Deer (whitetail and mule)
☐ Elk
☐ Lynx
☐ Moose
☐ Mountain goat
☐ Mountain lion
☐ Pika

Birds

☐ American dipper
☐ Common loon
☐ Bald eagle
☐ Harlequin duck
☐ Northern hawk owl
☐ Osprey (often confused with bald eagle)
☐ Ptarmigan

Reptiles and Amphibians

- ☐ Frogs (many types)
- ☐ Garter snake
- ☐ Long-toed salamander
- ☐ Toad
- ☐ Western painted turtle

FIRST-AID KIT CHECKLIST

Here is what we recommend for a very basic kit, all kept in a quart-size sealable plastic bag. Toss it in your backpack on all your hikes!

- ☐ Tweezers. This is for splinters; you may have some already, on your pocketknife.
- ☐ Safety pins. These can secure bandage wraps and be used to create arm slings, etc. Get larger ones that are robust—old baby-diaper pins are the best.
- ☐ Bandannas. These can be used for splints and slings, or dipped in water to cool off someone getting too hot.
- ☐ Adhesive bandages of various sizes and shapes
- ☐ Medical tape and gauze bandages for larger wounds
- ☐ Antibiotic ointment
- ☐ Antiseptic wipes
- ☐ Moleskin for blisters. Duct tape works just as well.
- ☐ Elastic bandage
- ☐ Medication. Ibuprofen or naproxen sodium, also called NSAIDs, help prevent swelling in addition to being pain relievers; antihistamine for allergic reactions; any prescription medications. For younger children, baby aspirin.

DAY-HIKING CHECKLISTS

The Ten Essentials

The point of the Ten Essentials, originated by The Mountaineers, has always been to answer two basic questions: Can you prevent emergencies and respond positively should one occur (items 1–5)? And can you safely spend a night—or more—outside (items 6–10)? Use this list as a guide, and tailor it to the needs of your family.

1. Navigation: Map, compass, GPS
2. Headlamp or flashlight, spare batteries
3. Sun protection: Sunscreen, lip balm, sunglasses
4. First aid: See above list for kit contents; be sure to include moleskin/tape
5. Knife or multi-tool, duct tape, twine
6. Fire: Matches or lighter, waterproof container, fire starter
7. Shelter: Rain jackets at a minimum, could include a tarp or bivy sack
8. Extra food: Sugary and salty, especially for kids
9. Extra water: Water bottles or hydration system, water filter or treatment
10. Extra clothes: Jacket, vest, pants, gloves, hat

Other useful items to consider

☐ Bear spray
☐ Day pack
☐ Toilet paper!
☐ Camera
☐ Binoculars
☐ Insect repellent
☐ Energy food

BACKPACKING CHECKLIST

☐ The Ten Essentials
☐ Bear spray
☐ Shelter (tent, tarp, bivy sack)
☐ Backpack with rain cover
☐ Toilet paper and a trowel (human waste should be buried at least six inches deep and 200 feet from water sources; toilet paper should be packed out)
☐ Ground cloth (to put under tent)
☐ Sleeping bags
☐ Sleeping pads
☐ Pillows or stuff sacks

- ☐ Whistle and signaling mirror
- ☐ Meals
- ☐ Energy food and snacks, especially for kids!
- ☐ Stove
- ☐ Fuel
- ☐ Cookset with pot grabber
- ☐ Dishes, bowls, and/or cups
- ☐ Utensils
- ☐ Bear canister or food bag and rope to hang food on pole
- ☐ Backup water treatment
- ☐ Spare clothing for number of days and for weather variations
- ☐ Permits
- ☐ Camera
- ☐ Binoculars
- ☐ Hand sanitizer and/or biodegradable soap
- ☐ Insect repellent
- ☐ Toothbrush
- ☐ Quick-dry towel
- ☐ Reading material, playing cards, other games and activities to keep kids entertained around camp

RESOURCES

PARK CONTACT INFORMATION

Glacier National Park, Park Headquarters, 64 Grinnell Drive, West Glacier, MT 59936; (406) 888-7800; https://www.nps.gov/glac

BEAR SAFETY

Bear Safety: http://igbconline.org/bear-safety
www.nps.gov/glac/planyourvisit/bears.htm

BOATING REGULATIONS

www.nps.gov/glac/planyourvisit/boating.htm

CAMPGROUNDS AND LODGING

Campground reservations

NPS campground reservations: www.recreation.gov
Backcountry campsite reservations: www.nps.gov/glac
/planyourvisit/backcountry-reservations.htm

Lodging reservations

Glacier Park, Inc.: PO Box 2025, Columbia Falls, MT 59912; (877) 403-0807; www.glacierparkinc.com

Granite Park Chalet: (888) 345-2649; www.graniteparkchalet.com

Xanterra Parks & Resorts: Inside the U.S.: (855) 733-4522; Outside the U.S.: (303) 265-7010; reserve-glacier@xanterra.com; www.glaciernationalparklodges.com

SERVICES

Boat trips and rentals
Glacier Park Boat Company: PO Box 5262, Kalispell, MT
59903; (406) 257-2426; www.glacierparkboats.com

Bus tours
Red Bus Tours: Inside the US: (855) 733-4522; Outside the US:
(303) 265-7010; www.glaciernationalparklodges.com/red-bus
-tours; reserve-glacier@xanterra.com

Sun Tours: PO Box 234, East Glacier Park, MT 59434;
(406) 732-9220 or (800) 786-9220; www.glaciersuntours.com

General: East side of the park
Glacier County Montana: http://glaciermt.com/St-Mary
Town of St. Mary: 4852 Kendrick Place, Suite 101,
Missoula, MT 59808; (800) 338-5072

General: West side of the park
Columbia Falls Area Chamber of Commerce: PO Box 312,
1402 E. 2nd St., Columbia Falls, MT 59912; (406) 892-2072;
info@columbiafallschamber.org

Horseback riding
Swan Mountain Outfitters: (406) 387-4405 or (877) 888-5557;
www.swanmountainoutfitters.com
May–September for same-day reservations:
  Apgar Corral: (406) 888-5010
  Lake McDonald Corral: (406) 888-5121
  Many Glacier Corral: (406) 732-4203
  West Glacier Corral: (406) 387-4405

Raft and whitewater tours
www.nps.gov/glac/planyourvisit/rafttours.htm

SPERRY CHALET UPDATES

https://glacier.org/newsblog/project/sperry-action-fund
/www.sperrychalet.com

TRANSPORTATION TO AND WITHIN PARK

Amtrak: www.amtrak.com/empire-builder-train
Glacier Park Express: http://bigmtncommercial.org/
Park shuttles: www.nps.gov/glac/planyourvisit/shuttles.htm

TRIP PLANNING

Authors' website: www.our4outdoors.com
The Big Outside: www.thebigoutside.com
Park maps and guides: www.nps.gov/glac/planyourvisit/maps.htm
Park website planning: www.nps.gov/glac/planyourvisit
/index.htm
Rocky Point Nature Trail Guide: www.nps.gov/glac/learn/
nature/upload/Rocky-Point-Brochure-web.pdf

WEATHER

National Oceanic and Atmospheric Administration (NOAA)
www.noaa.gov
www.weather.gov/
www.wunderground.com/

Even young kids can experience a sense of accomplishment in Glacier National Park. (iStock/saturated photo)

INDEX

ABOUT THE AUTHORS

Harley McAllister works as a project manager but is most alive when he is outdoors, especially with his wife, Abby, and their boys. He has lived in seven different states and on three different coasts, including four years with his family in the Dominican Republic teaching at a nonprofit school. Harley has rafted, skied, snorkeled, backpacked, mountain-biked, and camped in diverse locations in both North and South America. He has spent a lot of time off the pavement and loves to share his passions with others to inspire them to get outside more often, and have fun doing it.

Abby McAllister is a sometimes-harried mom of four boys, an outdoor enthusiast, a kitchen chemist, and copycat crafter. Together, she and her husband, Harley, have traveled the world, always seeking opportunities to get their boys out exploring nature. When she is not outside, she is busy writing books and blogs that will help other people get their kids unplugged and outside.

Get more travel tips at the McAllisters' website:
www.our4outdoors.com

OTHER TITLES YOU MIGHT ENJOY FROM MOUNTAINEERS BOOKS

Utah's Big Five National Parks: Adventuring with Kids

Harley and Abby McAllister

Family-tested and approved guide to Utah's five major national parks: Arches, Bryce, Canyonlands, Capitol Reef, and Zion!

Yellowstone National Park: Adventuring with Kids

Harley and Abby McAllister

The first volume in the *Adventuring with Kids* series is a guide to the world's first national park: Yellowstone National Park

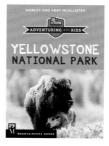

The Don't Get Lost Out There Deck

A deck of playing cards that also features tips for "staying found"